OA (pb)

Longman   York Press

Alan Pound is hereby identified as author of this work in accordance with Section 77 of the Copyright, Designs and Patents Act 1988

YORK PRESS
322 Old Brompton Road, London SW5 9JH

PEARSON EDUCATION LIMITED
Edinburgh Gate, Harlow,
Essex CM20 2JE, United Kingdom
Associated companies, branches and representatives throughout the world

First published 2001

ISBN 0–582–42458–5

Designed by Vicki Pacey
Phototypeset by Gem Graphics, Trenance, Mawgan Porth, Cornwall
Colour reproduction and film output by Spectrum Colour
Produced by Addison Wesley Longman China Limited, Hong Kong

ONTENTS

PART THREE

CRITICAL APPROACHES

PART ONE

INTRODUCTION

HOW TO STUDY A POEM

Studying on your own requires self-discipline and a carefully thought-out work plan in order to be effective.

- Poetry is the most challenging kind of literary writing. In your first reading you may well not understand what the poem is about. Don't jump too swiftly to any conclusions about the poem's meaning.
- Read the poem many times, and including out loud. After the second or third reading, write down any features you find interesting or unusual.
- What is the poem's tone of voice? What is the poem's mood?
- Does the poem have an argument? Is it descriptive?
- Is the poet writing in his or her own voice? Might he or she be using a **persona** or mask?
- Is there anything special about the kind of language the poet has chosen? Which words stand out? Why?
- What elements are repeated? Consider **alliteration, assonance, rhyme, rhythm, metaphor** and ideas.
- What might the poem's **images** suggest or symbolise?
- What might be significant about the way the poem is arranged in lines? Is there a regular pattern of lines? Does the grammar coincide with the ending of the lines or does it 'run over'? What is the effect of this?
- Do not consider the poem in isolation. Can you compare and contrast the poem with any other work by the same poet or with any other poem that deals with the same theme?
- What do you think the poem is about?
- Every argument you make about the poem must be backed up with details and quotations that explore its language and organisation.
- Always express your ideas in your own words.

This York Note offers an introduction to the poetry of Thomas Hardy and cannot substitute for close reading of the text and the study of secondary sources.

Why, in 1895, did the fifty-five-year-old Thomas Hardy turn his back on novel-writing and the London literary world, become a virtual recluse in his Dorchester home, and begin a second career as a poet?

Whatever the reasons which brought about these dramatic changes in his lifestyle and literary habits, Hardy certainly proved to be a prolific writer of poetry. Between 1898 and his death in 1928 he published over 900 poems, these being by his own account only a fraction of what he actually wrote. It is remarkable too that they included some of the greatest love poems in the English language: the series of **elegies** that Hardy, then aged seventy-two, wrote for his wife Emma after she died in 1912. Why, though, did this outpouring of love and grief also manifest such deep feelings of guilt?

Hardy is best known as the writer of **tragic** novels such as *The Mayor of Casterbridge* and *Tess of the d'Urbervilles*. But as soon as we start reading his poems we are obliged to re-examine many of our assumptions about him: their content and form, as well as the circumstances of their composition, disclose paradoxes and inconsistencies which this Note will address in more detail in subsequent sections. For instance, much of the continuing appeal of Hardy's poems, in an age even more sceptical than his own, is their universality. They deal with the things that are common to us all – birth, childhood, love, marriage, age and death – in honest, unsentimental, sometimes **ironic**, always thoughtful, and often moving ways. But they strike a chord in many readers precisely because of their lack of specificity and the absence of personal detail. Why, one wonders, is Hardy so reluctant to let us get close to him?

In fact, the poems are often less simple than they might at first appear, and Hardy himself remains an elusive presence in them. Indeed, much of the satisfaction to be gained from reading the poems comes from tracking the thought processes of the complex mind which lies behind them. Thus Hardy has a keen eye for the everyday experience of ordinary men and women in his poetry, but he is also profoundly aware of the mysteries of time and space, the forces of the universe which encompass human lives. Clearly, pessimism and **alienation** haunt Hardy's mind and poetry, but he offers – even as an old man – a determined resistance to them. The most memorable poems are those where Hardy seeks to restore human meaning and value to history and the landscape. How can we identify and, more crucially, how should we evaluate such material?

Hardy has often been seen as an anachronism, a **Victorian** who drifted into the twentieth century. This is misleading, even though the facts of his life story (see also Chronology) might suggest otherwise: born in a remote hamlet before the railway had pushed into Dorset; achieving a level of success as a novelist which gave him entry into the highest levels of Victorian society; and, finally, dying in the same year that Walt Disney released the first Mickey Mouse films. But the truth is that Hardy's attitudes were shaped during the 1860s and 1870s and these were the years when the modern sensibility was being shaped, when the cherished beliefs of Victorian culture – about religion, history, politics, gender, and so on – were crumbling, when Victorians began to see themselves as the victims rather than the masters of time, and as insignificant components in a vast and indifferent cosmic machine (see Themes and Historical Background).

Hardy is a complex figure because of his personal experiences and because he lived through turbulent times. Therefore we shouldn't, perhaps, be surprised to find contradictions and inconsistencies in his attitudes and outlook – but it is for these very reasons that he is such a fascinating subject. The assumptions of his rural upbringing were overlaid with the **ideologies** of Victorian middle-class culture, and both came into conflict with the radical ideas and attitudes he began to embrace as a young man. The tensions, even contradictions, which this gave rise to are evident in both his personal and his public life, and in his poetry. For example, he lost his faith but remained, according to his own account, 'churchy' all his life. He was an outspoken critic of Victorian middle-class society but he was eager to succeed in it. And although deeply pessimistic about the possibility of individual happiness, he continued to hope until late in life that the human race could make the world a better place (a hope which was destroyed by the First World War).

The mental turmoil of Hardy's formative years had a direct impact on the poetry he was to write some twenty years later. Indeed, it may be unlike almost anything else you have read. It mixes the simple and the sophisticated, the radical and the conventional, the familiar and the educated. It evinces feelings of loneliness and **alienation**, but strives to assert human meaning and value; it expresses dismay at the randomness of experience, while constantly searching for patterns; and, often written from the perspective of an old man, it plunders the past in order to revitalise the present. It employs specialised **verse forms**, as well as the more traditional ones found in **ballads** and hymns; and it mixes rural **dialect** with highly literary **diction**, often in the same poem. The sheer variety of Hardy's poetry, its spontaneity, and its wilful eccentricities – for Hardy thought polished writing was lifeless – are continually engaging.

Partly because of these qualities in his work, Hardy has been described as the first essentially twentieth-century poet. But one of the most attractive aspects of his poetry is that it is so difficult to classify. It is clear that he is unlike his Victorian predecessors in many ways. He rejected what he saw as their 'smoothness'. Equally, however, he doesn't seem to have much in common with the **modernists** such as T.S. Eliot and Ezra Pound, who were at the height of their powers before his death (see Literary Background and Critical History). We are not challenged by Hardy's poetry as we are by theirs to infer meaning from fragmentary forms, broken **images** and complex **allusions**. A much more illuminating way of seeing Hardy, and one which is examined in the discussions that follow, is as a major representative of a native English poetic tradition which has its roots in the **ballad** form and the oral tradition. This, for many readers, is precisely where Hardy's appeal as a poet lies.

PART TWO

COMMENTARIES

Thomas Hardy's *Collected Poems* were published after his death, in 1928, and contained over 900 poems (of which about sixty had been written before 1890). The majority of these had been published in eight separate volumes between 1898 and 1928.

With the exception of a handful of poems which often appear in **anthologies**, there has never been any agreement about what might constitute the core of Hardy's extensive poetic output. This is reflected in the varying contents of selected editions of his poetry. However, about thirty-five to forty poems regularly appear in such selections. If any consensus about a core of poems by Hardy can be reached, this seems as good a place as any to start – these recurring editorial choices provide the basis for the fifty poems discussed in the Commentaries which follow. They also reflect the range of Hardy's poetry and take account of poems he considered to be among his best. All eighteen of the original and essential *Poems of 1912–13* are discussed here, together with other poems meant to be read together ('The Five Students', 'The Wind's Prophecy' and 'During Wind and Rain'), as well as examples of Hardy's more public poetry.

All of the poems discussed can be found in *Thomas Hardy: Selected Poems* (1993) edited by Harry Thomas in the *Penguin Classics* series. This has a useful introduction and notes, and is the edition used in the preparation of this York Note. In accord with the principles of selection outlined above, these poems can also be found in *Thomas Hardy: Selected Poems* (1993) edited by Tim Armstrong in the *Longman Annotated Texts* series. This is an excellent scholarly edition which has detailed notes on each poem (including a very useful description of its **metrical** scheme) together with a challenging critical introduction. Armstrong also includes an appendix of excerpts from Hardy's notebooks, letters and autobiography. Finally, *Thomas Hardy: Selected Poems* (1998) in the *Oxford World's Classics* series, edited by Samuel Hynes, includes all but four of the poems discussed in the Commentaries. Again, this includes a good introduction and notes by a leading Hardy scholar.

NEUTRAL TONES

Hardy recalls a failed romantic affair; it was a first lesson in the disappointments of love

The poet recalls the specific moment when, on a bleak winter's day, he and his lover realised their relationship was over. He says that the particular scene has come to mind – almost as a personal **motif** of the hazards of love – when later relationships have run into difficulties.

The controlling **metaphor** of the poem, first announced in the title itself, is of a picture – or possibly an etching – in 'neutral tones'. The scene is drained of colour; the sun is described as 'white' and the few fallen leaves from the ash tree are 'gray'. This reinforces the key notion that the failure of the love relationship has drained the world of meaning: love dies (the woman's bored 'eyes', her false 'smile' and the inconclusive 'words' the lovers exchange confirm how things have changed) and this corresponds to the death of nature. To complete the idea, at the end of the third **stanza** a **simile** likens the 'grin of bitterness' which crosses the woman's face to an 'ominous bird'. The total effect of these details is to clinch the controlling metaphor: this dreary scene is inscribed on the poet's memory, and surfaces whenever he is again subject to love's 'keen lessons'.

The title also describes the poem's tone. For although the subject matter might have provoked an outpouring of feeling, this is in fact an emotionally restrained poem. Hardy keeps his feelings in check and, on the surface at least, tries to be objective. This kind of detachment is characteristic of Hardy. It is partly a self-protective manoeuvre, but it also shifts the poem into a more reflective mode, towards a consideration of the effects of the passage of time on human relationships. But the poem, which is generally very precise in its use of language, also evinces some awkwardness of expression, notably in the third stanza – what, for instance, does 'thereby' refer to? Such moments betray the real feeling just beneath the poem's surface.

On which lost the more on the question of which of us lost more

'I LOOK INTO MY GLASS'

In this poem Hardy reflects on the cruel irony that his ageing body still harbours the strong feelings of a much younger man

The poet looks in a mirror ('glass') and wishes that his feelings had decayed in the same way as his body. The distress he feels so acutely at the hostility of people he once considered friends has denied him a peaceful old age. In the final **stanza** he blames the arbitrary processes of time which have wasted his physical being while he remains mentally alert.

Hardy had lamented elsewhere the fact that human consciousness resides in the frail body. One consequence of his reading of Darwin (see Themes and Historical Background) was the belief that consciousness was almost an accident in a material universe, and that this was the source of much human woe. This relatively slight **lyric** only hints at the bitter personal experience which informs it – the distress arising from the negative criticism attracted by *Tess of the d'Urbervilles* and *Jude the Obscure* (see Thomas Hardy's Life) and Hardy's estrangement from his wife. The causes of Hardy's gloom in the 1890s are revealed in later poems such as 'In Tenebris' (I and II) and 'Wessex Heights'.

The opening **image** where the poet says he views his 'wasting skin' in a mirror is characteristic of Hardy's work, suggesting the adoption of a somewhat detached, reflective attitude towards his own predicament. This impression is further reinforced by the suppression of personal details, which (as in the previous poem) is in part a self-protective manoeuvre but which also has the effect of universalising the poem's treatment of the depredations of 'Time'. 'Time' is **personified** and thereby given a weighty and ominous presence in the poem – this contrasts with the **rhetorical** appeal in the first stanza to a God Hardy was unable to believe in.

The poem comprises four-line stanzas rhyming abab, in each of which lines 1, 2 and 4 are **iambic trimeters** and line 3 is an **iambic tetrameter**. This is a stanza form commonly used in hymns. Its deployment in such a sceptical poem has a clearly **ironic** effect.

frame body

eve the later years of the poet's life, the present, as opposed to the earlier prime of 'noontide'

DRUMMER HODGE

Assuming a more public voice than usual, Hardy writes (in reaction to much more jingoistic poetry of the time) about the poignancy of war, in this case the Boer War of 1899–1902. Hardy had read that one of the soldiers, a drummer boy killed and buried in South Africa, came from a Dorset village

Drummer Hodge, far from home and denied the normal funeral rites, is unceremoniously laid to rest in a crude grave. A native of rural Dorset and familiar with its topography and night skies, he now lies forever in an alien landscape beneath 'Strange stars'. Moreover the poem hints that 'homely' Hodge had only limited understanding of the forces of British imperialism which led to his death in South Africa, and may actually have felt a closer affinity to the Boer farmers he had been sent to fight.

The central **irony** of the poem – and the source of its poignancy – is that the simple country boy from Wessex is permanently transplanted to a foreign land. This is underlined both by the alien nature of the landscape in which he lies and, perhaps more significantly, by the unfamiliar (southern) constellations of stars which nightly appear in the sky over his grave. The use of Afrikaans terms in the first two **stanzas** – 'kopje-crest', 'veldt' and 'Karoo' – enhance the poignancy of the situation: not only is the landscape strange, but the local terms for it would have meant nothing to Hodge.

We do not, in fact, know the drummer boy's real identity – 'Hodge' was a slang word for an agricultural labourer, and had all the demeaning connotations of 'country bumpkin'. Hardy hated such terms and was very critical of those who used them. In the light of this, perhaps we can say that the poem is not centrally about the waste and futility of war at all – after the brutality of the first couple of lines this theme is not developed. Indeed, the exotic vocabulary, and the almost incantatory references to the foreign stars and constellations at the end of each stanza (reminiscent of the refrain often found in **ballads**) have a quite different effect: Hodge, who will forever be 'portion of that unknown plain', grows in stature, partly because his fundamental humanity is established in the face of the brute facts of the material universe ('strange-eyed constellations') and partly because of the growing sense of wonder associated with his death ('His homely Northern breast and brain / Grow to some Southern tree'). In affirming Hodge's uniqueness in this way, Hardy subverts the **stereotype** of the yokel – and the discriminatory ways of thinking which lie behind it.

kopje-crest the summit of a small hill
veldt open grazing land
Karoo flat, barren land
Bush uncleared land
gloam twilight

THE DARKLING THRUSH

Hardy's intellectual pessimism, which led him to believe that the only way to avoid pain in a universe of time and decay was to live in a state of 'unhope' (see 'In Tenebris I'), is called into question by the song of an old thrush which seems to suggest some cause for hope after all

The poem is set at the end of the day at the end of the year at the end of the nineteenth century (which, following much debate, had been officially dated as 31 December 1900). The overwhelming sense of things coming to an end in nature corresponds with the poet's dejected mood. The poem's detail reinforces this congruence. The poet is alone in a frozen, desolate landscape; night is closing in; the century is passing; and the poet is 'fervourless'. Suddenly an 'aged thrush' bursts defiantly into song, seeming to challenge all that has gone before. The surprised poet reflects on this. Does the thrush know something he doesn't? Is the poet's pessimism without foundation?

This is a poem which is richly suggestive in its choice of **diction** and deployment of **imagery**. The use of 'darkling' in the title, for instance, refers to both the thrush (which is literally in the dark) and the poet's state of mind. There is a literary **allusion** here too: in Matthew Arnold's 'Dover Beach' (published in 1867), a poem which deals with the loss of faith in the nineteenth century and the intellectual malaise prompted by evolutionary thinking, the poet compares the age to a 'darkling plain'. This idea is developed in Hardy's lines 'The tangled bine-stems scored the sky / Like strings of broken lyres', where the **simile** of the broken harps denotes the absence of joy and the collapse of faith. The funereal imagery in the second **stanza** is also striking. The description of the thrush in the third stanza is deliberately ambiguous: it is old and frail and in a sense emerges from the desolate landscape. Nevertheless, it sings lustily.

Critics have often said that the message of the poem is indeed that the bird knows more than the poet, that its song confirms that the poet's pessimism is unfounded – that there is 'Hope' which, if not presaging the return of God, at least anticipates the coming spring. However, a close reading of stanzas three and four makes this interpretation difficult to defend. The vigour of the thrush's song, though fully evoked, does not quite displace the melancholy picture which has gone before. Thus, while the thrush's 'full-hearted evensong / Of joy illimited' bursts upon the scene, the bird is nevertheless 'aged … frail, gaunt, and small, / In blast-beruffled plume'; and in lines which perfectly embody the tension between positive and negative, the bird is said to 'fling his soul / Upon the growing gloom'. The tentative **syntax** in the final stanza ('That I could think there trembled through') suggests that the poet remains unconvinced that there is any 'Hope'.

The overriding impression which the poem leaves is that the material world – here seen as an almost lifeless wasteland – remains utterly alien and threatening to the human consciousness (human beings merely 'haunt' this place). In later poems Hardy is more successful in projecting human value and meaning onto the landscape (see, for example, 'At Castle Boterel'). But here we find a perspective much more akin to Charles Darwin's view of nature (see also Themes and Historical Background): that it was a bleak place of struggle, without plan or purpose, but paradoxically also a site of astonishing creativity.

coppice   area of dense undergrowth and small trees
bine-stems   climbing stems of bindweed, perhaps jutting above a nearby hedge
outleant   laid out (as a corpse prepared for burial)

The self-unseeing

This poem recalls a happy moment from Hardy's childhood but he now regrets that he took it for granted at the time

Hardy remembers the cottage where he was brought up. While his mother sat beside the fire, the young boy danced to the music of his father's fiddle. It is a memory tinged with sadness: not only is his father now dead (he in fact died two or three years before Hardy wrote the poem) but on reflection Hardy realises that neither he, nor his parents, appreciated the fullness of the moment.

This is a beautiful little poem. The memory of the family scene is only sketched in, but the details are telling. Indeed, the effectiveness of the poem depends on its economy of manner: not only does the moment come alive but its poignancy in retrospect is given a universal resonance. The flagstones (of which the floor would have been composed) are described as 'Footworn and hollowed and thin', but the adjectives transfer to the human figures in the poem: the stones are almost as 'dead' as those who once walked on them. This is to be contrasted with the last **stanza** which is – until the chastening reflection of the final line – irradiated by the firelight from stanza two, as the memory and its meaning come into focus.

Alliteration (on the letters 'd', 'b' and 'g') plays a vital part in bringing this moment from the past alive. For one thing, it echoes the **rhythms** of the father's music and the child's self-absorbed dance. More specifically, in line 10 it draws attention to the word 'emblazoned', at first glance an odd choice (with its heraldic associations) in this context, but on reflection wonderfully apposite: picking up the blaze from the fire in stanza two, its suggestions of vivid and lasting colour give a particular resonance to the familial 'Blessings' of the moment described. The idea is completed with the suggestion that 'Everything glowed with a gleam' – not only literally, because of the light from the fire, but also figuratively, as in a painting which captures the extraordinary in an everyday domestic scene.

Hardy wrote elsewhere about his failure to apprehend fully the meaning of the present moment. He seems to have thought that this was a common problem and part of the psychic malaise of the times in which he lived. But here – although he sadly acknowledges the inevitable processes of time ('dream', 'that day' and 'gleam' all suggest the transience of the moment the poem has striven to evoke) – there is a triumphant reclaiming of the past and its significance in memory which is not only defiant of those processes but also a means of regaining the present. A similar thematic concern comes to fruition in the *Poems of 1912–13*.

IN TENEBRIS I

This is one of Hardy's darkest poems – the title is Latin for 'in darkness'. It was written in 1895–6, which was a period of personal crisis and depression for Hardy, and the poem reflects his black mood

Two of the sources of Hardy's depression are present in this poem: the estrangement from his wife (both 'my bereavement-pain' and 'that severing scene' **allude** to the death of their relationship) and the hostile reaction to *Jude the Obscure* (see Thomas Hardy's Life), including that of former friends who now 'turn cold'. Each **stanza** is self-contained and repeats the same pattern: nature is bleak, but the poet can no longer be affected by this because – and here is the dark twist – his own mood is even bleaker. In each case the faint hope is immediately dashed, and the poem moves towards the climactic 'unhope' and the final longing for extinction.

This is a disturbingly successful **lyric**, which skilfully deploys the **imagery** of winter: there is an accumulating sense of the death of nature and deepening darkness as the poem's constituent parts culminate in the 'Black … night', 'death' and 'unhope' of the final stanza. This is reinforced by the **metrical** pattern of the poem. The false hope is raised in the rhymed **iambic trimeters** of lines three and four in each stanza. But these are framed by the opening and closing

dimeter lines (also rhymed), where the heavy funereal stresses first announce the onset of winter, and finally snuff out any possibility of hope.

The poem provides a disconcerting insight into Hardy's mental condition in this period of his life. The bleakest aspect of the poem lies in the appalling sense that the poet is now beyond suffering – his heart has become, like the 'ancient pulse' in 'The Darkling Thrush', 'shrunken hard and dry', and he says he can suffer no more. Even in Hardy's work, such deep pessimism – here it is also a profound **alienation** – is rare: the tendencies are often present in his poetry but usually prompt a reaction, a struggle to reassert human value and meaning. In this case the reader must turn to the next poem to find the stirrings of resistance.

Percussus sum sicut foenum, et aruit cor meum 'My heart is smitten, and withered like grass' (Psalms 102:4)

dun a neutral, brownish-grey colour

smart hurt, but also possibly 'brighten up'

cope cloak

IN TENEBRIS II

In this poem Hardy enters into an imaginary dialogue with those who are optimistic about social progress. Out of this emerges an apology for his pessimism

The first three **stanzas** express Hardy's feelings of **alienation**: 'potent' voices proclaim that all is well with the world and he is made to feel out of step with the mood of the times. Finally, Hardy asserts his own position: human progress is possible but must continually struggle against the forces of evil, ignorance and prejudice, and not shrink from contemplating the problems of the world. But he still seems to feel that his is a discordant voice and that he must remove himself from society.

This is clearly a rather different poem from 'In Tenebris I'. For one thing, the longer lines indicate that Hardy is in a different mood, and is more willing to explain the causes of his mental anguish. These included the reception of *Jude the Obscure*, when he was condemned for a sincere attempt to grapple with the problems of society (see also

Thomas Hardy's Life). In spite of what his detractors have said, however, this poem makes it clear that Hardy did not consider the world to be a bad place. In fact, Hardy resented being labelled a pessimist, and preferred to be called an 'evolutionary meliorist' (see Themes). This entailed a refusal to close his eyes to injustice and cruelty which would otherwise never be remedied. The poem implies that it is possible to be happy in this world, but happiness is fragile and threatened by 'crookedness, custom, and fear' – that is, the ignorance, prejudice and obsolete social convention which he had exposed in *Jude the Obscure*.

Unlike 'In Tenebris I' this poem can hardly be described as a subjective **lyric**; rather, Hardy is putting forward a defence for his pessimism. The **rhetorical** trick he employs is to seem to give due weight to his critics' point of view (in the first three lines of each **stanza**) and denigrate himself (in the last), while actually steadily building his own case. In fact, the believers in social progress here emerge as brash, bullying, complacent, facilely optimistic, selfish and superficial. This is achieved by the mocking language and **rhythms** with which they are depicted: 'Breezily go they, breezily come; their dust smokes around their career'. After all this, Hardy's quiet, simple statement of his own position in stanza four, while on the face of it an admission of his ineffectiveness, is probably calculated to have quite the opposite effect: the reader could well applaud the fact that Hardy is 'shaped awry' and 'disturbs the order here' (a remark now heavy with **irony**) – that, in other words, he offers a dissenting voice.

swoln swollen

career occupation, but also 'reckless impulse'

A TRAMPWOMAN'S TRAGEDY

This is a ballad, based on a local story Hardy had heard. It develops one of Hardy's favourite themes: the anguish of reflection on words and actions which have brought unhappiness to others but, in a world ruled by time, can never be changed

The **narrator** and her companions – Mother Lee, Johnny and her lover – tramp through the countryside. In order to incite her lover's jealousy, the trampwoman flirts with Johnny. Angry, her lover asks whose child she bears, and on a whim ('to tease') she lies and says it is Johnny's. On hearing this, her lover stabs Johnny to death. For this he is hanged. Now alone and friendless, the woman gives birth to a stillborn baby. In a dream the restless ghost of her lover comes to her and asks whether the child was his or Johnny's. She tells him that after they became sweethearts she did not go with any other men. Satisfied, her ghostly lover then slips away from her forever.

This poem demonstrates Hardy's confidence in emulating the **ballad** form. The trampwoman's voice, the economical narration, the refusal to examine motive or apportion blame – all establish a feeling of authenticity, as do the skilfully contrived **stanzas**, the effective **refrain** and the **rhyme scheme**. But this story is quite explicitly set in Wessex (see Background on Hardy's Wessex): the detailed topography, particularly the careful listing of the countryside inns – many of them long since disappeared by the time Hardy wrote the poem – is much more specific than is traditional in ballads, and shows Hardy in another mode, that of the historian documenting a vanishing way of life. In this way Hardy places the events recounted in a changing locality and, very appropriately, in the context of passing time.

As so often in Hardy's poetry, time is a key element in this **tragedy**. In part, of course, the tragedy derives from the terrible consequences of what is really nothing more than foolish behaviour: the outcome is quite disproportionate to the initial actions and, **ironically**, quite the opposite of what the woman intended. But perhaps of greater interest to Hardy is the lifetime's anguish she will suffer because of her thoughtlessness. Even before the sudden death of his wife and the *Poems of 1912–13*, Hardy was aware of the torment of hindsight: if only we had known then what we know now, how differently we would have behaved! Here the woman's final dream-encounter with the ghost of her lover only serves to enhance this bitter recognition.

fosseway sunken road
turnpike toll road
landskip landscape
tap inn

tor and lea hill and meadow

settle wooden bench with a high back

Blue Jimmy a notorious horse thief who was active in Wessex in the early years of the nineteenth century; one of the horses he stole belonged to a neighbour of Hardy's grandfather

Ere his last fling he flung before he was hanged (at Ilchester jail in 1827)

CHANNEL FIRING

Published just four months before the beginning of the First World War, Hardy would later claim that this poem, with its sense of impending catastrophe, was prophetic

The noise of gunnery practice out at sea wakes the dead in a country churchyard. They think it is 'the Judgment-day' (when the final trumpet call will wake the dead and signal the end of creation). God tells them this is not the case but the gunnery practice shows that nothing has changed in the world since they were buried – countries are just as belligerent as ever. The dead reflect on this as they return to their rest.

This is a sardonic poem, its overt humour becoming a vehicle for a mordant comment on war and religion. There are several sources of humour: the irreverent portrayal of the dead (Parson Thirdly wishes he had not spent his life sermonising but had 'stuck to pipes and beer'), the startled reaction of the animals ('The glebe cow drooled'), the wry voice of God (who cracks – and laughs at – a joke of his own about damnation, and says he may defer the Day of Judgement forever, to give humanity a much-needed rest) – and all this **ironically** delivered in a form reminiscent of a hymn (**iambic tetrameters** rhymed abab).

But there seems to be a shift of tone in the last **stanza**. Indeed, a darker note may already have been struck in the fourth stanza when God refers to 'All nations striving strong to make / Red war yet redder'. The apocalyptic **imagery** perhaps betrays Hardy's premonitions about the European political climate. At the end of the poem the place names over which the noise of the guns roars their 'readiness to avenge' are carefully chosen. They are associated with three past civilisations: Stourton Tower was erected to commemorate the victory of King Alfred the Great of Wessex over the Danes in AD879; Camelot was the court of King Arthur, the semi-legendary king of the Britons around the sixth century AD; and Stonehenge is the prehistoric stone circle near Salisbury, believed to have been in use between 3100 and 1100BC. What is Hardy suggesting here? Perhaps that nothing has changed since the beginning of time, that human beings have consistently used a religious pretext for killing each other through the ages. Perhaps that God is just as bad as his people. Or even, perhaps, that human beings have created the God that suited their political and territorial ambitions – just as Hardy, in fact, has created a cynical God to suit his own purposes in this poem.

chancel the part of a church surrounding the altar and choir (usually the east end)

glebe cow cow grazing on church-owned pasture

Christés Christ's; is there any justification for this archaism other than a metrical one? Hardy's detractors have tended to highlight such usages as evidence of his poetic clumsiness – see Language & Style for discussion

THE CONVERGENCE OF THE TWAIN

Hardy wrote this poem for inclusion in a souvenir programme of an opera concert in aid of the *Titanic* disaster appeal. The White Star liner sank with the loss of 1513 lives on 15 April 1912 after it struck an iceberg

In the first five **stanzas** the poet imagines the great ship lying at the bottom of the ocean. He then explains that as the ship was being built, its fate was already being determined: the iceberg that would destroy it was also taking shape in the North Atlantic. The inevitable collision between the two takes place in the final stanza.

In the opening stanzas a striking contrast is established between the 'vaingloriousness' of the ship (its state-of-the-art engineering and its luxurious fittings) and the 'indifferent' marine environment. Later in the poem there are further contrasts. The construction of the ship is ironically counterpointed with the shaping of the iceberg by the 'Immanent Will' (for Hardy, the power behind existence: see the discussion of this concept in Themes). Who could imagine any connection between these 'Alien' events? But in the final stanza, the 'Spinner of the Years' (the Immanent Will in another guise) completes the web of fate and the pattern of the poem (which it brings full circle) when it decrees the collision of ship and iceberg. The forward movement of the verse is dramatically arrested by the heavy stress on 'Now!' and the following caesura, effectively mimicking the impact. This is the moment that the poem has been building up to. The shock is felt in the verse itself – partly because of the change of tense and the pauses which follow the phrases introduced by the repeated conjunction 'And'; partly because of the alliterative 'c' which evokes a juddering effect in 'consummation comes'; and partly because of the use of the word 'jars' itself, which awkwardly echoes the preceding rhymes ('Years' / 'hears').

Critics have disagreed on the theme of this poem. Some see it as an ironic condemnation of Victorian technological overreaching ('the Pride of Life that planned her'): at the time the *Titanic* was certainly considered to be the summit of engineering achievement, and its owners boasted that it was 'unsinkable'. Other critics have suggested that Hardy's real target was specifically the extravagance of the *Titanic*'s conception as a kind of floating palace for the rich (see stanzas III and IV especially). It is certainly true that after the disaster the ship's luxuriousness attracted much criticism – as indeed did the fact that more first-class passengers survived than those in steerage. Alternatively, other critics argue that the poem is not simply about human vanity (whether technological or self-indulgent), as this kind of interpretation does not take sufficient account of the workings of the Immanent Will in the latter half of the poem. Rather, the poem can be seen to be about the iron 'Necessity', as Hardy called it, which governs the universe. A fuller discussion of the themes, the language and the metrical patterns of this poem can be found in the Extended Commentaries.

stilly quietly
salamandrine the salamanders of legend were reptiles which lived in fire, but

Hardy probably, and ironically, means 'inextinguishable' here (the reference is to a red-hot iron used for lighting pipes, gunpowder, etc.)

thrid thread

bleared dimmed, blurred

august impressive, imposing

'When i set out for lyonnesse'

This poem was prompted by Hardy's visit in March 1870 to St Juliot, Cornwall, where he met Emma Gifford, who was to become his wife

Lyonnesse is the name for Cornwall in the Arthurian romances of Alfred, Lord Tennyson (*Idylls of the King*, published between 1842 and 1885), who in turn had taken it from Sir Thomas Malory (*Le Morte Darthur*, published 1485). In the first **stanza** Hardy sets out alone before dawn; the second states that neither prophet nor wizard could have predicted what would befall him at Lyonnesse; and the third describes his return – now in love and a changed man.

The apparent simplicity of this poem is deceptive. It is a version of a **rondeau**, one of the French **verse forms** which Hardy experimented with. It does not quite conform to the standard pattern, but the last two lines of each stanza repeat the first two, which is the main feature of the rondeau. Here the effect is both to raise the emotional temper of the poem, and to help establish Lyonnesse, or Cornwall, as a landscape of romance. The contrasts between the first and last stanzas draw attention to the transforming nature of the encounter with Emma which took place there. Initially the **narrator** is 'lit' by the stars, while on his return he is the source of illumination. Similarly, the mundane details (distance, frost) of his departure are replaced by the aura of magic and warmth which he exudes when he returns.

The poem is set entirely in Higher Bockhampton, Dorset, from where Hardy set out on 3 March to travel to St Juliot, Cornwall, to supervise the restoration of a church on the instructions of his employer. The poem does not take us to Lyonnesse/Cornwall, but the effect of this reticence is actually to evoke it as an extraordinary place

– remote, ideal, timeless, and capable of bringing about the magical transformations with which the poem ends. In the later *Poems of 1912–13*, in particular 'After a Journey', 'Beeny Cliff' and 'At Castle Boterel', Hardy, now an old man, journeys to Cornwall and endeavours to re-enter this landscape of romance in an attempt to recover from memory something of the mood recorded here.

rime frost

spray small branch or twig bearing flowers, leaves or berries

bechance happen

durst dared to

mute surmise silent conjecture

WESSEX HEIGHTS

This poem also belongs to that period of crisis and depression in Hardy's life (1895–6) treated in the 'In Tenebris' poems. Significantly, it seems to confirm his abandonment of novel-writing for poetry, and his withdrawal into seclusion in Dorset

Hardy says he has ascended the 'Wessex Heights', where he can be alone and free, to escape from the 'lowlands', peopled as they are by his critics, friends who have fallen out with him and (possibly) women with whom he has had failed relationships. He feels at odds with the world ('nobody thinks as I') – and, in **stanza** four, at odds with himself when he imagines his youthful 'simple self' lamenting the man he has become. Hardy wonders whether, after the personal and public pressures which have brought him to this crisis, he will be able to restore mental coherence by wandering the Dorset hills (and, of course, by writing poetry).

The locations of the poem are as much **symbolic** as real: Hardy may be marking out his poetic domain (see Background on Wessex) but the contrast between the lowlands (where the novels, particularly *Jude the Obscure*, got him into so much trouble with critics – see Thomas Hardy's Life) and the highlands (where he is free to write his poetry) tells us more about his state of mind. There is a pause for bitter reflection in stanza four, where Hardy says that the 'chrysalis' of his youthful self failed to fulfil its promise. Certainly the 'continuator', that is, the middle-aged man who succeeded the youth, proves in the huge **couplets** and leaden (mainly **iambic**) **rhythms** of this poem that, in his depression and lack of will, he is now anything but a butterfly.

There has been a good deal of speculation about the identity of the women in this poem – none of it very conclusive. They may be real women, or characters from Hardy's novels, or a combination of the two. Perhaps the most noteworthy thing about them is their ghostliness: here, Hardy wants to keep the 'ghosts' at 'their distance' (stanza eight) – it is a measure of his depression and **alienation** – but in later poems he will actively seek to re-engage with them and his past.

mind-chains the conventional attitudes of Hardy's critics (William Blake's 'mind-forged manacles' in the 1792 poem 'London' come to mind)
weird uncanny, supernatural

The following eighteen poems comprise the famous sequence of **elegies** that Hardy wrote following the death of his wife Emma. You can find a critical overview of the sequence in Critical Approaches. The Latin **epigraph**, '*Veteris vestigia flammae*', is taken from Virgil's **epic** *Aeneid* (first century BC) and means 'traces of the old flame'.

THE GOING

This is Hardy's first attempt to come to terms with the shock of Emma's death. Ironically, it has reawakened all his old feelings for her

Hardy asks his wife why she gave 'no hint' of her imminent death, which has 'altered all'. He recalls the days of their courtship – and then we learn that his anguish is sharpened by the estrangement in the latter years of their relationship. But nothing can be changed now – and she will never know how her death has affected him.

The striking aspect of this poem's tone is the way it shifts backwards and forwards between remorse and irritation. Alongside the grief at Emma's death, we hear echoes of the couple's marital squabbling. 'Why did you give no hint ...' he chides her from the start. This bitterness is perhaps at its most chilling in the second **stanza**: the reiterated complaint that she slipped away without a word of farewell ('Never to bid good-bye / Or lip me the softest call') almost seems to suggest that she died to spite him, to get her own back for his harshness towards her, which lasted until the moment of her death (as the rather odd use of the word 'harden' to describe the daylight in line 11 reminds us). But there are other ways in which Emma's 'great going ... altered all' and any bitterness is offset by his sadness – the difficult realisation that he will never see her again, the agony of his reviving love for her, and his feelings of emptiness. His anguish is superbly conveyed at the close of stanza three, when for a moment ('a breath') he thinks he sees her strolling, as used to be the case, between the trees at dusk: 'Till in darkening dankness / The yawning blankness / Of the perspective sickens me!' Following this we learn of the way their relationship deteriorated. In stanza four there is a glimpse of Emma as she was at the time of their idyllic courtship in

Cornwall: the 'red-veined rocks', with their fleshy overtones, are associated with her and suggest how she was then full of youth, life and vigour and completely at one with that romantic landscape. Stanza five returns to the present and we realise that the note of irritation in the poem probably derives from self-reproach: in addition to the sorrow at her passing there are feelings of guilt, for both the animosity of recent years and, latterly, the neglect of her suffering. As a consequence the poem's tone modulates, after all, into forgiveness and tenderness – although the faltering **rhythms** and broken **syntax** of the final stanza betray the despair which undercuts this.

In view of the title, it is revealing to examine the various uses of the verb 'to go' in this poem, since they help plot the progress of Hardy's pain and serve to invest Emma with unique qualities. They certainly underline the notion of movement and travelling which is characteristic of the whole sequence of the *Poems of 1912–13*. This perhaps denotes travelling *in time*, which is the lot of human beings and a source of sorrow in this poem and elsewhere in Hardy's work – a view of life as a journey subject to time and change. Hardy is perhaps lamenting the impossibility of revisiting the past to change things in the light of new awareness, specifically here the realisation of Emma's centrality to the plot (as Hardy saw it) of his life. In later poems in the sequence Hardy will attempt the difficult task of travelling back in time in an attempt to reclaim the past, even if he cannot 'amend' it.

Some critics have found the form of the poem to run counter to its emotions – a **metrical** 'box' into which Hardy has had to force his meaning. The problem really centres on lines five and six of each stanza: unlike the other lines, which tend to echo the **rhythms** of speech, these **iambic dimeter** couplets with **feminine endings** could sound incongruously light and tripping. This is perfectly acceptable in stanza four – where the context (the ecstatic courtship days) justifies the tone – but is more surprising elsewhere (e.g. 'Where I could not follow / With wing of swallow'). One could argue that the abrupt change of tone in fact sharpens the poignancy of the poem. Alternatively, it has been suggested that the heavy stresses in these lines actually work against the insubstantial rhymes. Perhaps Hardy wishes to emphasise that, contrary to what many may think, poetry in fact offers no simple consolation, or therapy, to those suffering real emotional torment.

lip me give voice to (with suggestions perhaps of a ghostly kiss)
beetling projecting, overhanging

YOUR LAST DRIVE

Hardy continues to register his shock at Emma's sudden death. This is a calmer poem than 'The Going' and is sometimes seen as a prelude to recovery. The balance has shifted more towards sympathy for Emma, but Hardy's self-reproach is explicit

Hardy reflects that Emma had no idea, on what was to prove to be her last drive, that she would never again see the 'borough lights' (of Dorchester); nor, as she passed the churchyard (of Stinsford), that she would shortly be laid to rest there forever. The last two **stanzas** review their relationship: Emma's reproachful 'words' recall the harsh things he said to her while she was alive. But they also record the simple new fact: she is dead, and will never know whether she is still hated, or whether his love for her has been reawakened (as in fact is the case, sadly only now that she is gone).

Although the tensions evident in 'The Going' are still present, Hardy now seems to feel more tenderness than animosity towards Emma. **Ironically**, now that she is dead he is 'closer' to her than he has been for years. He calls her 'Dear ghost' – the odd collocation suggesting why the pain is so intense. The unassailable fact of her death is effectively communicated in the reference to the 'flickering sheen' of Emma's face on that last drive: she was so recently infused with life, but now that mysterious spark has been extinguished and she is a corpse. Moreover, the word 'flickering' is ambiguous, carrying suggestions of transience, which in this context hints at premonition.

Hardy doesn't spare himself in this poem. He says that even if he had been with Emma on that last drive, he would have failed to notice 'the writing upon [her] face'. He does not, of course, mean that her fate was inscribed on her face – but in a sense that *his* fate was. If only he had had the wit to anticipate how he might feel upon Emma's death, if only he had treated her better while she was alive. 'If only …' he had known then what he knows now he would have avoided all this anguish and guilt. Having been drawn into a dialogue with Emma's ghost – and the illusion that it is still possible to seek Emma's forgiveness – he finally accepts the reality of the situation, and the poem ends with a bleakly despairing **couplet**:

> Yet abides the fact, indeed, the same, –
> You are past love, praise, indifference, blame.

THE WALK

Hardy is still preoccupied with the suddenness of Emma's death. The 'difference' between then (when she was alive) and now (that she is dead) is starkly evoked. But it is more difficult to judge his mood in this poem

Hardy describes his habitual walk, often taken alone recently because of Emma's illness. He has taken the same walk again since her death but now he is 'alone' in a quite different sense and he tries to define what that difference is.

Again, Hardy uses the idea of a journey. His walk is both real – the actual route which he was accustomed to take – and **metaphorical** – that space of time during which Emma died and things were never the same again. The poem is carefully structured to suggest an outward journey, leaving behind a familiar setting, and a return to a room which is the same yet not the same – a room with an absence, an emptiness. That is the 'difference'.

In this poem, any impulse to blame Emma has gone. There doesn't seem to be any self-reproach here either. These absences, together with the orderliness of the poem and its restraint, are often interpreted as evidence that Hardy has achieved a measure of calm, a further stage in his recovery. But the very same features could also be seen as evidence of the despair which follows shock in traditional **elegy**. The reality of Hardy's anguish, whatever the outward (poetic) appearance, can perhaps be judged by the change of **rhythm** in the final terse **couplet** – that is, the forced pause after 'sense' and the

THE WALK continued

largely **anapaestic** final line (when earlier long lines have been mainly **iambic**). Certainly this is a 'return' with a 'difference', both **metrically** and emotionally.

RAIN ON A GRAVE

In this poem Hardy conforms to elegiac conventions. It is often seen as representing a significant step towards his recovery but perhaps doesn't have the conviction of other poems in the sequence

In her grave, Emma is exposed to the winter rain from which, when living, she would have been quick to shelter, even in a Cornish summer. Bleakly acknowledging that there is now nothing he can do to protect her from the elements ('arrows of rain'), Hardy wishes he could exchange positions with her – or join her in the grave, as life means little to him now. Finally, he affectionately recalls her childlike delight in nature and observes that she will become absorbed in its cycles through the daisies which will blossom on her grave in the spring.

Hardy incorporates several of the conventions of the traditional **elegy** in this poem (see also the discussion of the *Poems of 1912–13* in Critical Approaches). The tears of the bereaved are linked with the rain which falls on the grave; in turn, this rain nourishes the flowers on the grave as Emma is taken up into the natural processes, which promise a new spring to follow the winter of death and mourning. Traditional elegy often employs the **motif** of flowers growing on a grave, as well as the **image** of rebirth, as Emma becomes a child again at the conclusion of the poem.

This poem has attracted a good deal of criticism. For one thing, Hardy does not challenge elegiac convention as he does, more or less explicitly, in other poems in the sequence. What is missing, therefore, is that emotional authenticity which often derives from Hardy's resistance to the standard forms (and easy consolations) of traditional poetics. In this respect Hardy seems to have a surprisingly sentimental view of nature in this poem. Equally, the lilting **rhythms**, which derive from both the two heavy stresses in each line, and the preponderance of **feminine rhymes** ('lay there' – 'away there' – 'stray there' – 'day there', for example, in the third stanza) seem strikingly incongruous. The rhythms of this poem are reminiscent of nursery rhyme – but it is perhaps too ingenious to suggest (as some critics have done) that this is meant to build towards the final stanza and capture something of Emma's vitality and youthful enthusiasm for life. Hardy's intention seems to have been twofold: firstly to see Emma more objectively – it is the first time he has referred to her as 'her' rather than 'you'; and secondly to reaffirm a harmony between them after the ambivalence of the previous poems. Perhaps the point is that at this stage he can do neither with much conviction, and lapses into the conventional.

dust-paven rills dusty channels through which the summer rain trickles

'I FOUND HER OUT THERE'

This poem anticipates the pilgrimage Hardy will make in later poems to the scenes of his courtship of Emma. Cornwall is established as a landscape of romance and Emma a figure who properly belongs there

The poem describes how Hardy met Emma in Cornwall ('Lyonnesse') and then brought her back to Dorset, where she now lies buried. He reflects that she is far from the country she loved, the space of her youth, her vitality and her dreams. He imagines her ghost stealing westwards to hear again the sound of the Atlantic waves which once gave her so much joy.

The poem's effectiveness lies in its use of contrasts. The reality of Dorset, where Emma lies buried, is contrasted with Cornwall, that place of romance which is far away. This is also a contrast of time, of course: *then*, when Emma was young and full of life, and *now*, when she is a corpse. Cornwall is a place of wind and crashing breakers, while Emma's Dorset grave is 'noiseless'; Cornwall was a place of freedom for Emma, but now she lies in her 'loamy cell'. And the point is of course that she was fully at home in Cornwall, and partook of its natural characteristics. Thus, for example, the sun 'Dyed her face fire-red' there, implicitly drawing attention to her sexual vitality.

This poem seems less concerned with expressing Hardy's bereavement-pain (although it is present, as is the continuing note of self-reproach) than with trying to capture the essence of Emma. The poem concludes with an **image** of rebirth characteristic of the **elegy** (see also 'Rain on a Grave'): Emma's ghost hears the Atlantic waves and is resurrected 'With the heart of a child', a quality which was uniquely hers. Finally, part of the picturing of Emma in this poem depends on the representation of Cornwall as a landscape of romance. Its remoteness and wildness are stressed, but more subtly it is seen as a place of stories and legends: its cliffs are 'haunted', Dundagel head is 'famed', and, poignantly, Emma herself 'would sigh at the tale / Of sunk Lyonnesse'. But just as the myths of Lyonnesse belong to a fabled past, so too does the love story of Emma and Thomas Hardy – for it was engendered in that romantic place but later fell victim to the realities of time and circumstance.

loamy cell grave
Dundagel Tintagel (associated with King Arthur)
Lyonnesse north-west Cornwall (see 'When I Set Out for Lyonnesse')
domiciled lived

Without ceremony

After the experiments with more conventional elegy, Hardy returns to the manner of the opening poems of the sequence. However, he seems to have moved beyond shock at Emma's death

Hardy recalls that Emma had a habit – after friends had visited, when planning an excursion to town – of slipping off without a word. This was the manner of her death, too, and he conjectures that she couldn't be bothered in life or death to say 'Good-bye'.

There is no suggestion of apportioning blame here: Hardy's attitude towards Emma – who he calls 'my dear' – seems to be tender throughout. He does not invoke any of the **motifs** of conventional **elegy** here. Indeed, this is a strikingly matter-of-fact poem compared with the two preceding ones. The deliberately unpoetical qualities of the writing – the **rhythms** of speech, the everyday **diction**, the absence of **imagery**, the understated patterning of the poem (notice how the **rhymes** of the first lines in each **stanza** are limited) – all contribute to a kind of poignant domestication of Emma's death. Hardy's self-reproach is related to this process. He now realises that his inference that she couldn't be bothered to say 'Good-bye' was wrong; rather, it was the consequence of his animosity towards her. The poem quietly affirms the importance of saying 'Good-bye', but it is too late to change anything now.

'Quietly' is the keynote of this poem. In emotional terms, it is strikingly restrained. Hardy's style is characteristically reticent, but even by his standards this poem is remarkably spare. Perhaps what the poem doesn't say is more important than what it does: is there a grudgingly painful realisation that his inference was wrong? More generally, the tone of the poem is finally balanced between resignation and despair.

LAMENT

This poem constitutes a further exercise in conventional elegiacs. It depends for its effect on the sad perception of Emma's exclusion, now she is dead, from all the things that she enjoyed in life

A garden party, a dinner party, the first stirrings of spring – these are the things Emma enjoyed, but now she is confined to her grave. The final **stanza** declares that those who survive her are unable to enjoy these things either, now that she has been taken from them.

This poem represents a variation of conventional **elegy** known as a **lament**. In each of the first three stanzas, snapshots of Emma in life are generated, only to be erased in the final four lines. The pattern varies slightly (but appropriately) in the fourth stanza, where the effect of her absence on those who remain is recorded – to be followed by the final blunt confirmation that she is 'dead / To all done and said'. As in ' "I Found Her Out There" ', the poem exploits contrasts: then she was full of life, now she is dead; then she was in the light, now she is in the dark; then she was free, now she is confined forever in her 'tiny cell'. The poem is keen to stress Emma's vitality, and again records her childlike enthusiasm ('With a child's eager glance'), in this case for people as well as nature. However, in a further contrast, these things seem 'stale' to those who remain. Visually, the pattern of each stanza narrows to the finality of the grave in which 'she is shut'.

'Lament' can be compared to 'Rain on a Grave' and ' "I Found Her Out There" '. In all three poems there is a wish to see Emma more objectively – she is addressed in the third person on each occasion – and to capture her unique qualities. These are also suggested by the informal and lively **rhythms** of the first seven lines of each stanza. This pattern is abruptly forestalled in the seventh line with the pause and (in three of the stanzas) the uncompromising monosyllable 'But'. Thereafter the tone is quite different: the rhythm slows because of the heavy stresses and the triplets create the impression of a sombre refrain. In the final stanza Hardy finds himself alone even in the company which delighted Emma – but which now simply bores him. Here is confirmation indeed that she has gone. The poem lurches between the consolation of memory and the blank despair of present reality – but as a consequence there is an emotional authenticity here which is lacking in the earlier elegies.

rime frost
Candlemas-time the Feast of the Purification of the Virgin Mary (2 February)
tranced entranced (the intransitive form of the verb 'to trance' also has an earlier sense meaning 'to die')
junketings feasts, picnics

THE HAUNTER

This poem amounts to wish-fulfilment but it seems appropriate at this stage of the sequence. Hardy imagines that Emma's ghost lovingly haunts him

Emma's ghost can be neither seen nor heard by Hardy but she is with him constantly, responding to the desolate appeals of the earlier poems. She reflects on the changes in their relationship – the early shared love of nature, the later estrangement – and the way her death has revived his love for her. She hopes that her ghostly presence may save him from despair and give him the will to go on living.

For the first time in the *Poems of 1912–13* Hardy gives a voice to Emma's ghost. He imagines her saying all the things he longs to hear. That this is a complete fiction is underlined by the fact that Hardy cannot hear her: she addresses the reader and we are urged to tell 'him' that she is a benign ghost who wishes to heal him with her love and fidelity. This raises the whole question of the sense in which Hardy can be said to 'hear' the dead Emma's voice at all, which will be taken up again in the next poem, 'The Voice'. Here, the fact that this is a fantasy sharpens the reader's sense of Hardy's desolation: if only he *could* hear her! But that would be a scenario of romance and not reality, which the **ballad**-like echoes of this poem **ironically** hint at.

Finally, the representation of Emma's ghost in this poem is problematic. She seems remarkably forgiving – or is it simply that the impulse to view her wholly sympathetically (after the earlier irritation) has now developed? In the second **stanza** she touches on the central irony of the whole sequence: that Hardy wants her more now than he did when she was alive. But she is very even-tempered about this, showing little sense of reproach. It is worth comparing this ghost to the one that appears in later poems, for example 'After a Journey' and 'At Castle Boterel'. In this poem Hardy acknowledges his wife's finer qualities – but ultimately this cannot alleviate his guilt: Emma is dead, and, ironically, communication between them fails here as it did when she was alive.

THE VOICE

This is perhaps the bleakest of all the poems in the sequence. Paradoxically, though, it does mark a real turning point after the earlier false starts: following this Hardy begins the process of recovery, and soon will make the trip to Cornwall where he met and fell in love with Emma over forty years ago

Hardy hears Emma's voice calling him, saying that she has reverted to her earlier self which he loved so much. But is it really her he hears? He hopes that he will again see her as he did in Cornwall in the earliest days of their courtship. But already his confidence that he *can* hear her has gone. Perhaps, after all, it was only the sound of the breeze. Emma is gone forever and he is an old man.

This poem further explores the issue raised in the previous poem: can Hardy hear his wife's voice or not? The poem is constructed to register his growing doubts about this: the relative excitement of the first two **stanzas** gives way to the growing uncertainty of the third and the bleakness of the fourth. In fact, the doubts are already present in the second stanza: Hardy recalls Emma waiting to meet him in her 'air-blue gown', an unusual adjectival compound which perhaps does communicate her youthful vitality, but more poignantly suggests that this particular ghost already has the potential to disappear. And this is what happens in the third stanza, where the vision fades: the voice modulates into the breeze, and the ghost dissolves to 'wan wistlessness' – that is, becomes pale (ghostly) and, paradoxically, both wistful and unwitting ('wistlessness' is a coinage, or **neologism**, on Hardy's part). In the final stanza Hardy writes that the woman is still 'calling', not now because he expects to actually hear her, but in order to express the unbearable longing for her which he will feel until he himself dies.

The **metrical** effects of this poem are striking. The voice of the woman coming and going on the breeze ('is it only the breeze?') is suggested by the **dactylic tetrameters** employed in the first three stanzas, the **triple rhymes** (e.g. 'call to me', 'all to me') on lines one and three, and the abrupt truncation (they are two syllables short) of the other two lines. In the final irregular stanza the metre breaks down completely: basically **trochaic**, there are three stresses in lines 13 and 14, four in line 15, and possibly only two (depending on how it is read) in the final line. In effect the **rhythm** stumbles, emulating the 'faltering' steps of the aged speaker as his hopes of seeing his phantom-wife are dashed.

The landscape is also used to enhance Hardy's emotional desolation at the end of this poem. The vision of youthful Emma in her summery attire forty-two years before fades and Hardy again sees before him the dead winter landscape of present reality. 'Listlessness' is the key word here, ostensibly describing the breeze, but more applicable to Hardy's state of mind at the end of the poem, after the earlier – but momentary – respite. The emphasis on the effects of change and decay in nature serves to remind us of the same processes at work in human experience: 'Leaves around me falling, / Wind oozing thin through the thorn from norward.' The falling rhythms (**dactyls** and **trochees**) of the poem's penultimate line vividly evoke Hardy's downward spiral into the despair of the final line, where – now in his mind only – the woman is still 'calling'.

Paradoxically, however, a closer look suggests that there is also something more positive going on in the poem. There are glimpses of the young Emma of their courtship days, and an attempt to displace the more recent version of her. The poem seems to present Hardy at his lowest point, but it contains the seeds of recovery (however ambivalent that recovery might prove to be). The process we see here is developed in later poems with the pilgrimage to Cornwall and the reclaiming of an idyllic past.

H IS VISITOR

This is the second – and last – occasion when Emma speaks in the sequence. Again, the issue of whether Hardy hears her ghost is touched on here – but perhaps more importantly, this poem marks the final 'departure' of the older Emma from Max Gate and Hardy's pursuit of her younger self in Cornwall and the past

The ghost of Emma rises from her grave and slips through the gardens and rooms of their home. She notices all the changes that have been made since her death, and the new servants she does not know. She is upset and announces that she will return to her grave and never visit the house again.

Here Hardy has transferred the contrast between what is and what used to be (clearly delineated here once again) into the mouth of Emma, which suggests that it will never again be as painful as it has been in earlier poems. Indeed, there is a kind of burying of the older Emma going on in this poem: the final short lines of each **stanza** (with two **stressed** syllables) seem to consign her to oblivion ('the roomy silence'), where she rejoins the anonymous 'Souls of old'. Hereafter Hardy will seek out the youthful Emma in memory.

There is an emotional ambivalence about this poem. There is certainly a poignancy in imagining the ghost revisiting her old home and noticing the changes. But the reader may not be sorry to see the last of the older Emma. She has nothing to say about her husband (this in itself could be revealing) but is instead preoccupied with the domestic changes at Max Gate, the Hardys' home since 1885. This also again raises the question of whether Hardy actually hears Emma. It is easy to assume that she is addressing her husband ('you') here, but she could well be speaking to the reader, as in 'The Haunter'. Emma does not speak after this in the *Poems of 1912–13*: in 'After a Journey', for example, Hardy says he comes to 'view a voiceless ghost', and the vision he summons up from memory will be of Emma as young, vital and passionate.

Mellstock the name given to Stinsford (where Emma was buried) in Hardy's fictional Wessex (see also Background on Hardy's Wessex)
softling quiet and gentle
manifold many, various

A CIRCULAR

This poem might almost be seen as an ironic comment on the whole sequence of the *Poems of 1912–13* which are, similarly, messages which will never be delivered as the intended recipient is dead

Hardy, as Emma's 'legal representative', opens her mail and finds a brochure for ladies' spring fashion. But the lady for whom it was meant was buried last winter, 'costumed in a shroud'.

In some ways this short poem typifies Hardy's outlook on life: he attaches great significance to moments like this and seems to derive, as the final line suggests, a grim pleasure from them.

In formal terms, the poem attempts to catch something of the stilted, formulaic **diction** of the brochure ('in tints as shown',

'Warranted up to date'). In fact, Emma is as dead as the language in the brochure. Perhaps Hardy is quietly expressing an anxiety of his own – that words may betray the dead, and Emma in particular, by failing to capture the essential life that was once theirs (see the reference to the 'flickering sheen' of Emma's face in 'Your Last Drive', and 'her life's sheen' in the next poem in the sequence). This possibility is a matter of concern to him as he prepares for the pilgrimage to Cornwall and the poetic envisioning of Emma at the time of their courtship.

A DREAM OR NO

This poem marks a turning point in the sequence. Hardy considers undertaking a journey to Cornwall and the scenes of his courtship with Emma many years ago. He wonders if this is perhaps the way to come to terms with her death

Hardy wonders whether St Juliot in Cornwall, where he first met Emma, holds the 'key' to his life (and the bereavement-pain he has felt). Surely it does, for he has often thought of her at that time and their meeting so many years ago. But then doubts overwhelm him: did that young woman ever exist? Indeed, do St Juliot and the other scenes of their courtship exist?

The title, the opening questions and the **diction** of the first four **stanzas** ('necromancy', 'fancy', 'dreams', 'dreamed') anticipate Hardy's doubt, which is more clearly articulated towards the end of the poem: was his love for Emma, and their idyllic courtship, just a dream? Interestingly, even as the doubt is being formulated, the young Emma with whom he fell in love begins to surface in memory and words. And the questions which conclude the poem anticipate the decision to undertake a pilgrimage to Cornwall and track Emma 'through the dead scenes' (as the next poem, 'After a Journey', puts it) in order to prove her reality.

The question then becomes: what does that 'reality' amount to? This poem gives an indication as to the answer – and also the difficulty of the endeavour. Hardy has already struggled with the notion of giving a voice to Emma – from now on the attempt will be to represent the essence of the younger Emma in the poetry, to conjure up a vision of the beautiful, vital young woman she once was. The process begins here but the effort of consciousness (that is, in memory and language) required will be considerable: Emma was once and perhaps still is 'in hiding', 'lonely', and 'other than nigh things uncaring to know'. Has he the mental and poetic resources to represent her 'life's sheen', to capture those almost indescribable qualities that made her uniquely Emma, and not betray the dead?

necromancy the art of conjuring up and communicating with the dead in order to predict the future

AFTER A JOURNEY

The poems set in Cornwall – in particular this one, 'Beeny Cliff' and 'At Castle Boterel' – form the core of the sequence. The issue at stake in all three is the effort to reclaim the past as a way of resisting the processes of time and change

Hardy follows the ghost of the youthful Emma to the scenes of their courtship in Cornwall forty-three years before. Has she reflected on the way their relationship deteriorated after its idyllic beginnings? That cannot be changed, however, and the implication therefore is that this return to the past might offer some comfort. Hardy urges the ghost to bring him again to these locations as he claims he is 'just the same' as he was all those years ago.

This is a stunning poem – some readers would say the central poem of the sequence (though 'At Castle Boterel' also has a claim to this status). What is so impressive here is the effort of consciousness, of memory and language, to challenge the brute facts of the material world: on the one hand, the processes of time and change (the passage from summer to autumn defines the decay of the relationship in **stanza** two: 'Summer gave us sweets, but autumn wrought division'); and on the other, an indifferent universe (the physical presence of the landscape is striking in this and the other core poems: consider, for example, the onomatopoeic qualities of the 'unseen waters' ejaculations'). The poem wishes to assert that the human mind, which understands loss, lack and insignificance, is also capable of reclaiming the past and imposing human value on the landscape.

In Hardy's mind the waterfall, and the cave (which 'seems to call out to me from forty years ago'), will always be associated with Emma and with those romantic events which took place many years before but which are vividly present both in memory and landscape 'now'.

But how successful in fact is Hardy in reclaiming the past here, and in defeating time? Some critics say that the vividness with which Emma is imagined confirms that love has indeed triumphed over time in this poem. This view is problematic, however. Hardy *almost* captures Emma in stanza one (this is denoted by the description of her here: 'With your nut-coloured hair, / And gray eyes, and rose-flush coming and going') but she remains elusive. By the third stanza, even though the memory is briefly vivid, Emma is reduced to a 'thin ghost' and Hardy is left only with the mocking echo from the cave (suggested by the **feminine rhymes** and **alliteration** on 'l': 'hollow', 'call', 'all aglow', 'frailly follow'). And throughout there is the curious sense that Hardy is talking not to Emma but to himself. This is because he cannot forget that she is actually dead and that before her death he was on very bad terms with her. This is especially evident in stanza two, where the sombre tone is as much a product of the **diction** ('years', 'dead scenes', 'past', 'dark space', 'lacked', 'division' – and the ambiguity of 'twain', not simply 'two' but 'divided') as of the rhythms. Indeed, the last line seems to suggest that time holds the upper hand here. So this first attempt to envision the youthful Emma (Hardy says he has come here in order to 'view a voiceless ghost', having renounced all hope of dialogue with her), to reclaim the past, and to assert a love which might defeat time, ends not in serenity but in disappointment and bitterness. This is confirmed in the final stanza: an indifferent nature offers no comfort, and daylight erases the last possibility of vision (the ghost returns to the grave). It has been suggested that the final lines of this poem show the triumph of conviction (and therefore of vision) over the realities of time and change. But surely the jarring rhyme ('lours'/'flowers') undermines Hardy's assertion that he is 'just the same' as he was in those far-off, idyllic days – as a consequence the poem ends, in fact, on a note of despair.

lours looks sullen

A DEATH-DAY RECALLED

This is a poem which looks back to the sudden shock of Emma's death. But it belongs with the core Cornwall poems because it hints at the struggle of consciousness to impose human value on indifferent landscapes, which is one of their central themes

The Cornish landscape which Emma had loved so much in her youth – and longed for during the difficult Dorchester years – was completely indifferent to the hour of her death. Hardy expresses astonishment that it evinced no sign of shock or mourning.

A convention of pastoral **elegy** has Nature mourning the loss of a loved one for whom the poet grieves. In this poem, however, Hardy's complaint that the places Emma loved in Cornwall did not mourn for her is an affectation: Hardy dismissed the '**pathetic fallacy**', the poetic conceit that Nature can feel as humans do, and in this respect followed John Ruskin (who invented the phrase). There is much in this poem which confirms that Hardy is mocking this particular elegiac convention. Above all, the light, tripping **rhythm** of the poem (deriving from the hymn **metre**, the **feminine endings** on alternate lines and – particularly in stanza one – the abundance of **alliteration**) are inappropriate for such an elegy. Moreover, the welter of **personifications** (and their failure in every case to evince any emotion, for example 'Beeny did not quiver') and the self-conscious **periphrasis** (for example, 'creamy surge', 'limpid store') mockingly imitate the high-flown language of conventional elegy. Finally, the **rhetorical** questions in the last stanza do not serve to add weight to Hardy's complaint (as they should in conventional elegy); on the contrary, in this context the reader might be inclined to take the issue up with him!

Nevertheless, the poem has a serious intent too. For one thing, the landscape was as oblivious to the approaching death as Hardy himself (which is now a matter for self-reproach). Perhaps even more important for the poet at this stage is the need to underline the indifference of nature to human concerns, a fundamental belief of Hardy's, but one which motivates his wish to restore (human) meaning to the landscape – which he does in the core poems of this sequence by tracking the ghost of the woman he loved.

purl rippling and bubbling
limpid clear

Beeny cliff

Forty-three years have elapsed since Hardy's first visit to Beeny Cliff, when he was courting Emma. Although he vividly recalls the earlier occasion, he now stands there alone and seems more reconciled to the processes of time which have brought about this change

Hardy excitedly recalls the time he visited Beeny Cliff with Emma. It provided a beautiful backdrop to their courtship, part of the idyllic quality of the day (they hardly noticed the changing weather). Now many years later, the cliff seems a more ominous presence. And whatever memories it holds for him, the reality is that Emma is now dead and it means nothing to her.

Each **stanza** is self-contained but, with the third stanza as a pivot, the poem contrasts 'then' and 'now', as do many of the *Poems of 1912–13*. The first two stanzas recall the scene in 1870 through both sight and sound. The opening line is striking: 'O the opal and the sapphire of that wandering western sea'. Here the long, rhythmic line, the description of the colours of the sea in terms of jewels and the unusual use of 'wandering' to portray its movement are very effective. The tone set is one of exhilaration, and thereafter the lovers – Emma in particular – are vividly evoked. The scene changes in stanza three. There is a shower, and the Atlantic is briefly overcast. The lovers seem oblivious to this slightly darker note, but it provides a transition to stanzas four and five – away from memory (however reluctantly) and into the sadness of the present. The shift is marked by the changed aspect of the landscape: the cliff retains its 'chasmal beauty' but in stanza four it 'bulks' and in stanza five it 'looms'. Nevertheless, in Hardy's thoughts it seems to take second place to the fact that 'The woman now is – elsewhere –', the hesitation communicating all the more effectively the painful recognition that Emma is dead.

The stanza form is unusual – **iambic** (for the most part) **heptameters** with **rhymes** in triplets. But it is the facility with which Hardy manipulates the **rhythms**, often in conjunction with **alliteration**, within this framework that is impressive. In the first two stanzas in particular, the long, fluid lines with their effortlessly modulating rhythms generate a sense of excitement and identification between the lovers and the landscape on that day long ago. The alliteration on 'l' in line six clinches this: '... laughed light-heartedly aloft ...' Alliteration on 'd' and 'l' in stanza three adds an ominous dimension to what is only a passing rain-cloud which temporarily darkens the ocean, but which as a consequence casts a shadow over the rest of the poem: 'And the Atlantic dyed its levels with a dull misfeatured stain'. Stanza four opens with a pause denoting a transition to the realities of the present and a change to slower, less flexible rhythms. This is immediately confirmed by the alliteration on 'b' in line ten, which now endows the cliff where the lovers once frolicked with a sinister aspect: 'Still in all its chasmal beauty bulks old Beeny to the sky'. After the opulence of earlier lines, the monosyllables which enunciate the questions of lines eleven and twelve bring out Hardy's despair. In stanza five, strong and meaningful pauses frame the word 'elsewhere'. The final line, with its heavy rhythm and hollow, echoing sounds, seems drained of hope.

The unspoken question at the end of the poem is: where is Emma now? In effect this is the question that all the core poems of the sequence ask. Here, the answer seems to be that she exists in Hardy's memory, forever associated with the sites of their courtship. But unlike 'After a Journey', there is no pretence that time can be defeated. The 'resurrection' of Emma in the opening stanzas is counterbalanced by the courageous recognition later that she is, in reality, dead.

In this poem Hardy gives equal weight to vivid memory and present reality. But it is perhaps worth noting that in order to achieve this balance, Hardy has resorted to a significant omission. Nothing is allowed to compromise the representation of the blissful lovers. Drawing on the conventions of romance, the poem asserts that all they had to fear was time and death. And to do this, as readers of the preceding poems know, Hardy has had to quietly suppress the truth about the deterioration of his subsequent relationship with Emma.

mews seagulls
plained complained
prinked adorned, dressed up
main ocean

AT CASTLE BOTEREL

This is arguably the greatest poem not only of the 1912–13 sequence but of all Hardy wrote. It comprises a powerful effort in consciousness to defeat the processes of time by reclaiming the past, but even here there is an undercurrent of loss and guilt

Hardy seems to be on the point of leaving Cornwall and the scenes of his courtship of Emma. He glances back at the hillside and in his mind's eye he sees himself and Emma as they were forty-three years before: was there ever, he asks, a 'time of such quality … In that hill's story?' Emma is now dead but in Hardy's memory her 'phantom figure' remains on that hillside. However, as his own death approaches, he bids farewell to her ghost and the landscape of romance.

The challenge for Hardy here is to convince the reader that the subjective memory can transcend the objective facts of *time*, by reclaiming the past, and of *space*, by putting human meaning back into the landscape. Hardy's bold ploy is to mention the rocks which border the road, on the face of it suitable **symbols** for the indifference of both time and space, as they outlast the 'transitory' (that is, the human) 'in Earth's long order'. But the amazing thing is that even they bear traces of the presence of the courting couple all those years ago – they 'record … that we two passed' (compare a similar idea in 'The Shadow on the Stone').

One might argue that this is just a fancy, but it helps to underpin that culminating vision of Emma, the 'phantom figure' which remains on the hillside in defiance of both the passage of time and the materiality of space (or landscape). This constitutes a powerful expression of faith. The various poetic effects which conspire to make us want to believe Hardy are discussed more fully in the Extended Commentaries, as is the critical proposition that love does indeed conquer time in this poem.

Castle Boterel   Boscastle harbour
chaise   lightweight open carriage
balked of   denied

Places

In the preceding poem, Hardy recalls scenes from Emma's youth in Cornwall. Here, while those recollections remain vivid, he casts his mind further back to her childhood in Plymouth, Devon. This poem, in contrast to the Cornwall poems, illustrates the dangers of a journey into the past – it may overwhelm the present

No-one thinks of Emma's birth in Plymouth over seventy years ago; no-one thinks of the little girl lying in bed listening to the nearby church bells; and no-one thinks of the young woman riding recklessly over the hill near her new home in Cornwall. No-one, that is, except Hardy, who seems to find these scenes more real than the present.

After the great poems tracking Emma 'through the dead scenes' (see 'After a Journey') as a means of recovery from the pain of bereavement, this poem seems emotionally to be something of a throwback to earlier poems in the sequence which record Hardy's despair. There is still a return to the past, but this is not entirely memory and the apparent reminiscences seem curiously second-hand – which they are, the details coming from Emma's **memoir**, *Some Recollections*. There is, then, an unconscious **irony**, for Hardy's complaint in the poem is that it is the *present* which feels second-hand to one for whom memories have 'a savour that scenes in being lack'. The description of Emma as a child is unremarkable ('little girl of grace' and the 'sweetest the house saw') and she is linked, somewhat conventionally, with natural beauty ('like the bud of a flower'); perhaps more significantly, she is associated with a vanished way of life, as **symbolised** by the church bells, now silenced, to which she used to listen when lying in bed. These events, we are told, took place in 'the hollow of years ago' – an **image** which suggests not only how they have been almost erased by time but also how determined Hardy is to burrow into the past.

Stanza three draws on Hardy's own memories of Emma during the courtship years in Cornwall ('here'), since he had seen her riding on Boterel Hill himself (although again the details are from her memoir). And this stanza certainly evinces more vitality and conviction than the previous two (Emma's 'airy flush outbid / Fresh fruit in bloom'). However, following the vision of Emma's childhood, this more personally-felt recollection seems to trigger in Hardy a mood of utter desolation: 'to-day is beneaped and stale, / And its urgent clack / But a vapid tale.' Poetically, this is superior to almost everything that has gone before: Hardy can find nothing of interest in the present, for all its noise and bustle. The image suggested by the 'urgent clack' is that of a train clattering noisily, but purposelessly, over railway tracks. The characteristic sound of the carriages in motion is echoed in the **rhythms** of the final two lines. There is also a criticism here of what Hardy saw as the frenetic meaninglessness of the twentieth century, into which he felt, as an old man, he had strayed. He often used the railway as a **symbol** of an anti-human progress which was destructive of an older and better way of life – both Emma and the days of their courtship belonged to that former time. However, Hardy's attempts elsewhere to reclaim the past usually have the virtue of providing a basis for a renewal of the present. But here the dangers of tracking through the past are clear: the dead can stifle the living.

Three Towns Plymouth, Stonehouse and Devonport (after the pilgrimage to Cornwall, Hardy visited Plymouth, where this poem was written)
beneaped (of a ship) kept aground or in harbour by a neap tide, where there is little difference between high and low water
vapid insipid, lacking interest

THE PHANTOM HORSEWOMAN

This poem marks the end of the sequence of *Poems of 1912–13* as Hardy originally conceived it. Although he continues to feel the pain of bereavement, he now seems reconciled to the fact of Emma's death

The poem describes an old man on a Cornish beach in a grief-stricken reverie. It is said he sees not the scene before him, but one from many years ago: a phantom horsewoman. And he sees this vision constantly, even when far from this seashore. Although he grows older, the 'ghost-girl-rider' is ageless – and will haunt that landscape as long as he lives (and the poem exists).

It is significant here that Hardy refers to himself in the third person ('a man I know'). And even though the man sees 'as an instant thing / More clear than to-day' a scene which took place on this shore long ago, there is (as a consequence of that detached narration) no possibility here of Hardy falling into the same morbid frame of mind as in 'Places'. Since he also announces, as the man 'turns to go', another kind of detachment – from Emma's ghost in Cornwall (even though he carries the vision with him) – the reader can assume with some confidence that Hardy has regained a measure of psychological balance after the earlier grief. However, his mind is not entirely untroubled – the man on the beach 'stands / In a careworn craze', suggesting not only grief but the fact that Hardy still feels guilty about his treatment of Emma in the years before her death. But in terms of **elegy** Hardy has reached the end of the **cycle** of mourning.

Crucially this involves an ability to distance himself from the dead woman, and replace her with a **symbolic** alternative, a 'phantom of his own figuring'. In effect, it can be argued that the generation of an ideal **image** of Emma – a vision of his wife as she once was – has been Hardy's objective in all the core Cornwall poems. Its source, in a striking fusion of subjective and objective, as Hardy's consciousness invests the physical image of the youthful Emma with the power to resist the meaninglessness of nature and time, is clear in this poem. And the vision – 'drawn rose bright' on his mind – is triumphantly evoked: consider in this respect not just the visual descriptions of Emma, but the **rhythms** of the whole poem, imitating the ebb and flow of the tide, and building to the thrilling last line (with its **anapaests** and **internal rhyme**) when the phantom 'Draws rein and sings to the swing of the tide.'

In a careworn craze   disturbed with grief
alway   (archaic form) always

[**End of the** *Poems of 1912–13*]

E XEUNT OMNES

> **The title means 'all retire' and is a stage direction for the actors at the end of a scene or play. On his seventy-third birthday, Hardy reflects on the fact that he still lives while so many of his friends and relatives have died**

Hardy imagines himself standing alone at the site of a country fair when everyone else has left. He reflects on the desolate scene. The fair-goers have dispersed at twilight into the mist and soon he will follow them.

> The effectiveness of this poem depends in part on the deployment of the fair as a **symbol** for the transitoriness of human life. It is almost as if Hardy is surprised to find himself the sole lingerer/survivor when everyone else has gone/died. The description of the empty and littered fair-site is an **objective correlative** for Hardy's mood and situation: emotionally empty ('an air of blankness') and nearing death himself (the environs 'Wizen themselves to lankness'). The concluding **image** of the folk fading into 'the clammy and numbing night-fog / Whence they entered hither' is a striking representation of the mysterious and (in Hardy's view) godless eternity bordering finite human lives.

> Much of the emotional force of the poem depends upon the fact that Hardy is not simply reflecting on the conditions of existence, but thinking specifically of the passing both of people he had loved and of a way of life with which he was familiar. He now awaits his own death, and the poem thus occupies a moment suspended between public and private extinction.

> This tension between life and death is reflected in the **metrical** effects of the poem, reinforced by the **rhyme scheme** and **diction**. In each stanza the more optimistic rising **rhythms (iambics** and **anapaests)** of the second and third lines are framed by the falling rhythms (**dactyls** and **trochees)** of the first, fourth and fifth lines. Thus the more positive rhythms fail to make much impact, often themselves faltering. In the first, fourth and fifth lines of each stanza the **feminine endings** reinforce the dominant falling rhythm of the poem – its metrical tendency to 'wizen', 'dribble' and 'fade' – and the **double**

rhymes (for example, 'whither'/'hither'/'thither' in the final stanza) clinch the point. These effects emphasise the way in which the here and now soon become yesterday: the fair seems to dissolve before the reader's eyes as Hardy reflects on the transience of existence and his own imminent death. Thus the poem's form perfectly embodies its characteristic Hardyean theme: the representation of the processes of time and decay as the fundamental conditions of existence.

Wizen shrivel
Kennels gutters

HEREDITY

After reading Darwin, Hardy was very interested in the idea of heredity. It raised for him the uncomfortable possibility that we might unknowingly inherit traits from our ancestors which could have fatal consequences

The voice we hear is that of the 'family face', speaking for the inherited characteristics which are passed from generation to generation even though the individuals that bear them die. It is often difficult to pin down these characteristics which determine resemblance, but they are, paradoxically, immortal.

Here is something 'in man' which is 'eternal', which can defy the processes of time. Inherited characteristics leap across the years and generations while 'Flesh perishes'; they 'Despise the human span / Of durance' and refuse to die. Hardy **ironically** plays off the 'eternal' nature of inherited characteristics in this poem against the normal human perceptions of time and change. And he points up the further irony that these enduring features are so elusive, surfacing in 'curve and voice and eye', but always amount to a recurring likeness. The voice of the 'family face' we hear is appropriately vigorous, confident, even cocky and mischievous – perhaps something of a malign sprite.

It has been suggested that Hardy really does see these inherited characteristics which survive individual lives as evidence of the eternal in human beings – a kind of Darwinian version of Plato's theory of 'forms', that is to say, the unchanging, timeless forms which underlie, but shape, everything in the everyday, transient world of experience (see also Themes and Historical Background on Hardy's interest in Darwinism). But this is surely much too optimistic a reading of the poem: rather, Hardy sees heredity as another cruel trick played on the individual in a Darwinian universe, further evidence of our lack of freedom, for we are bound to reproduce the characteristics and traits of our ancestors. It is known that Hardy believed himself to be the last representative of a dying family, cursed by some inherited (but obscure) blood-legacy.

anon following

NEAR LANIVET, 1872

In a letter to a friend, Hardy said that the events described here took place when he was courting Emma. They are therefore prophetic of the unhappiness she was to suffer in their marriage

Out walking with Hardy, Emma rests on a handpost. Hardy is dismayed to notice that her pose suggests the **image** of the Crucifixion. The thought has struck Emma too and she is despondent. Hardy tries to reassure her but both wonder if it is an omen of future misery for her.

In Holman Hunt's painting *The Shadow of Death*, which Hardy knew, the young Christ yawns with arms thrown back and casts a shadow of the cross on the wall of his father's carpentry shop, prefiguring his fate. It is an example of **Victorian** typological art, a form of biblical interpretation that saw some events as proleptic, that is, anticipating those to come (most commonly, certain events in the Old Testament were interpreted as foreshadowing the life of Christ in the New Testament). This was a way of demonstrating God's providential plan for the world. Hardy had lost his faith – and he specifically rejected the notion of a divine purpose – but such thinking continued to hold an appeal for him. This is because he was enough of a Victorian to still long for evidence of *pattern*, both in his own experience (as in this poem) and in the universe generally (see the further discussion in Themes). The incident near Lanivet takes its place as a premonitory event in the pattern of Hardy's life, which is not fully disclosed until

Emma dies and the centrality of his love for her is confirmed (as the *Poems of 1912–13* make clear).

Hardy's wish to locate this event in a larger narrative dictates some of its characteristic features. The incident described took place forty-five years before the poem was written, but is recounted in the light of the following years of marriage and the unhappiness which it can now be seen to have foretold. The sombre tone of the poem is in part generated by its **metrical** form. The rhymed **quatrains** are reminiscent of **ballad** form, but while the second and fourth lines are fairly regular, there are five free stresses in the first and third lines. In keeping with a story yet to be told, the ballad metre is therefore incomplete, and the longer lines with their broken **rhythms** tend to drain the poetry of its vitality – matching the physical tiredness of the lovers, and hinting at future trouble in the relationship.

The mood of the poem is reinforced by the **diction**, which is unrelentingly dark: 'twilight-time', 'dim-lit', 'dusty', 'murked obscure', 'solitude', 'shade'. Moreover, the lovers are 'tired', 'weary', 'sad' and 'wordless'. Night falls, echoing the darkness of the crucifixion, and the death of love is anticipated. The final line of the poem contains a full stop and a long pause which gives a particular emphasis to 'Alas, alas!' as Hardy reflects despairingly on the intervening years.

Finally, although the poem seems to forecast future unhappiness for Emma, consider the implications of Hardy's unconvincing reassurance in line 25: ' "There's nothing in it. For *you*, anyhow!" ' A reading of the *Poems of 1912–13* helps to clarify what Hardy is getting at here: Emma's crucifixion – the pain he caused her while alive – will become a cause of acute remorse for *him* after her death.

glass hourglass

THE OXEN

> This poem records a folk tradition Hardy had heard from his
> mother. It is somehow the more poignant because of its first
> publication (in *The Times* on 24 December 1915) during the
> course of a brutal world war

It is midnight on Christmas Eve, and one of the older members of the
group around the fireside says that the oxen are kneeling, as they have
always done at that time. The listeners picture the scene, although such
beliefs are unfashionable now that religious faith is in decline. And Hardy
(non-believer though he is) says that, if asked, he would go to the remote
farmyard where the animals are in the hope that it might be true.

This poem is informed by nostalgia for a lost faith and lost beliefs –
perhaps, too, lost childhood and a vanishing rural community life.
Yet all this is suggested by very simple means, which themselves
contribute to the poignancy of the poem. The act of faith of the first
two **stanzas**, which is also a reclaiming of the past, is gently
undermined by the scepticism of the present in the second half of the
poem. The change hinges on the description of the belief as a 'fancy
few would weave' nowadays, that it is a fiction with no basis in fact.
But it is an appealing fiction, and it is significant that Hardy awaits
the invitation to test its truth (in a remote farmyard remembered from
childhood) while knowing really that no-one will ask – thus not quite
closing the door of doubt on it.

It is worth examining the **metrical** plot of the poem as it moves from
past (in stanzas one and two) to present (in stanzas three and four).
Essentially, the poem conforms to the 'common metre' found in
ballads and hymns: **quatrains**, made up of alternately rhymed **iambic
tetrameters** and **trimeters**. But there are variations here, notably the
lilting **anapaests** in the first two stanzas, which underpin the
nostalgia for the past (e.g. 'An elder said as we sat in a flock'), and the
more rigorous iambics of the second two stanzas, reinforced by
alliteration (e.g. 'So fair a fancy few would weave'), which denote
the shift to a more sceptical present.

barton farmyard
coomb short valley or deep hollow

THE LAST SIGNAL

**The Dorset dialect-poet William Barnes was buried on
11 October 1886. Barnes had encouraged the younger
Hardy's literary ambitions**

As Hardy approaches the graveyard where Barnes's funeral is under way,
the plaque on the coffin catches a ray of the sinking sun; the flash stands
out vividly against the sombre cloud in the east. Hardy interprets this as a
farewell 'wave' from his friend and mentor.

> It would be a mistake to find evidence in this poem of a belief in the
> workings of the supernatural. Hardy does not suppose for one
> minute that the dead man has actually communicated with him –
> the only messages here are Hardy's own. But Hardy's consciousness
> has been stimulated by the accidental reflection to imagine a
> moment of human communion in the face of time, death and nature.
> The process is very similar to that going on in the core Cornwall
> poems of the 1912–13 sequence. As in those cases, where the
> communication is in reality only one-way, the dead find ways of
> breaking their silence.
>
> The poem also picks up an anxiety of Hardy's expressed in
> 'A Circular'. The 'sudden shine' is not only the gleam from the coffin
> lid; it is also **symbolic** of Barnes's uniqueness as an individual human
> being when alive. Might poetry betray the dead by failing to faithfully
> reproduce their 'shine'? One of the ways Hardy seeks to be faithful to
> Barnes here is by emulating his use of the **metrical** patterns of ancient
> Celtic poetry, for example, **rhyming** words at the end of a line with
> those in the middle of the next (such as 'road' in line 1 with 'abode' in
> line 2, and 'meant' in line 9 with 'sent' in line 10) and the use of
> consonantal patterns within individual lines (such as 'The sudden
> shine sent from the livid east scene'). Moreover, Barnes's enthusiasm
> for the techniques of Anglo-Saxon verse is echoed in the poem's use
> of **alliteration** ('Something flashed the fire of the sun that was facing
> it, / Like a brief blaze on that side') and exploitation of compound
> epithets ('yew-boughed', 'grave-way') – a feature of Hardy's craft
> which he had largely acquired from Barnes. But the attempt to
> capture Barnes's 'shine' is not restricted to his poetic accomplishment:

the coffin lid which flashes as it reflects the 'brief blaze' from the sun momentarily calls to mind Barnes's gregarious nature, and specifically 'a farewell ... signalled ... As with a wave of his hand'.

THE FIVE STUDENTS

This is the first of three major journey poems (the others are 'The Wind's Prophecy' and 'During Wind and Rain'). In each case the journey motif provides Hardy with the opportunity to reflect on the course of his life, tracing patterns in his own experience. In this poem, he meditates on the deaths of four people who were close to him (though in reality they were never together like this)

On a late spring day, Hardy and four companions stride purposefully forth. In high summer one of the company drops out. Autumn comes and still the walkers press on, until another member of the group falls by the wayside. As winter approaches there are only two left. By the end of the year, only Hardy remains on the road – but he knows that he too must give up shortly.

Despite the title, the course followed here is not an academic one but life itself. The **metaphor** of life as a journey is a common one; here it is linked to the changing seasons (compare this with the passage of time in 'Afterwards'). The consequence is a sense of the remorseless march of time and its toll on the living. The word-portraits of the seasons in each **stanza** are detailed and effective – partly because Hardy was a man who 'used to notice such things' (as he says of himself in 'Afterwards'), and partly because, like Darwin (see Themes and Historical Background), he was impressed by the paradox that nature was both a place of struggle and death, and a site of vitality and endless variety.

Perhaps this paradox also accounts for the complex **metrical** pattern of the poem: only the second and fourth lines of each stanza have the same number of **feet** (they are **iambic trimeters**; the other lines in each stanza are, in order, iambic **tetrameters**, **pentameters**, **hexameters** and **dimeters**). This variety allows for much flexibility of **rhythm** in the poem and provides for a tension between positive and negative cadences which matches the thematic tension between vitality and death. The early lines in the first four stanzas are vigorous, both rhythmically and lexically, suggesting a correspondence between the energies of nature and the determination of the 'students'. The rhythm slows, however, in the **refrain** (reminiscent of **ballad** form) with its **incremental repetition** in line five, which in every case records loss. The tone is much more sombre and reflective in the final lines of each stanza and arrests the forward drive of the preceding lines.

Time triumphs in the final stanza as death closes in on Hardy. Winter claims the landscape ('Icicles tag the church-aisle leads') and throughout the stanza the heavy, leaden rhythms match the deathly scene. Indeed, the rhythm threatens to collapse entirely in the final line. 'One of us' (Hardy himself) alone remains – and after an emotional pause comes confirmation that all the others are 'gone', the deferral of the word until the end of the line giving it an awful finality. The terse concluding words of the poem, with their grim pun on 'rest' (suggesting both 'remainder', i.e. Hardy, the last of the travellers and soon to die himself, and 'release' from the pain of loss), are actually very eloquent in communicating Hardy's desolation.

Five Students scholars have disagreed on who they are: 'dark he' was identified by Hardy as Horace Moule (d. 1873 – see 'Standing by the Mantelpiece') and 'fair she' is almost certainly Emma Hardy (d. 1912); 'dark she' could be either Tryphena Sparks (d. 1890) or Helen Holder (Hardy's sister-in-law, d. 1900); 'fair he' may be either Henry Moule (Horace's brother, d. 1904) or Hooper Tolbart (an old friend of Hardy's, d. 1883). The fifth student is of course Hardy himself
beating tramping
on the beat both 'walking on' and 'performing daily habits'
anon to follow soon

THE WIND'S PROPHECY

Unlike the previous poem (or the next) this poem looks forwards rather than backwards. It describes Hardy's first journey to Cornwall in 1870 where he was to meet and fall in love with Emma Gifford. Oddly, perhaps, the poem is filled with foreboding

Hardy journeys across a hostile landscape thinking of the dark-haired city lover he has left behind in the east. The wind mockingly tells him he is yet to meet the fair-haired seaside woman in the west who will displace her in his affections.

Hardy here undertakes another **symbolic** journey, which again demonstrates the effects of time and change. Each **stanza** repeats the same pattern: a description of the landscape is followed by a dialogue between the poet and the wind. Indeed, the wind seems almost to mock him (this is the effect of the **internal rhyme** in the seventh line of each stanza). On one level, the striking scenic descriptions confirm Hardy's view of the universe as hostile, or at best indifferent, to human beings. Here the point is reinforced by the application of mechanical qualities to it. At the beginning of stanza three, for example, nature is seen in terms of industrial processes. But we begin to realise that the turmoil is in Hardy's mind as much as the landscape, or at least, they are in a tense dialogue with each other.

With this in mind, it is instructive to note the number of times in the poem that natural events are given human characteristics (or **personified**). If this is taken to emphasise the link with Hardy's state of mind, we can infer that he is subject to forces over which he has no control. And perhaps he *does* want us to believe that the plot of his life – the marriage to and subsequent estrangement from Emma (hindsight and guilt also inform the mood of this poem) – was mapped out already for him in 1870; and writing in 1917 he can see this emergent pattern clearly. This poem can therefore be regarded as providing an example of the working of an 'iron Necessity' in the affairs of human beings (see also Themes).

ebon ebony

terrene terrain
Huzza cry
vulturine vulture-like
Skrymer giant in Norse mythology who snored so loudly that the god Thor and his companions feared they were in the midst of an earthquake
pharos lighthouse

DURING WIND AND RAIN

This poem describes scenes from the life of a family, finally revealing that the participants are now all dead. It is a deeply ambivalent poem which may, or may not, contrive to extract some human consolation from a world of change and decay

Family singing, work in the garden, breakfast on the lawn, and a move to a new house – all are seen in the context of time's destructiveness. When the storm which has been gathering in the poem breaks, it is over the graves of the family members.

The scenes of family life described in the poem derive from Thomas Hardy's memories and Emma Hardy's **memoir,** *Some Recollections.* In the first three **stanzas** there are affirmative accounts of family fellowship (the singing), work (clearing the path, building a seat) and leisure (breakfast on the lawn). The family members lead their lives with an easy assurance and a sense that they will go on forever. They move house (in stanza four) but take this confidently in their stride. Nevertheless, this scene does denote a change in their lives and provides a link with the recurrent **symbolism** of wind and rain (that is, the destructiveness of time) with which the family activities are counterpointed throughout the poem. Each stanza ends with **images** of destruction as the 'years' take their toll, and finally the rain is described running down the inscriptions on their tombstones.

This is an ambivalent poem which has prompted different critical interpretations. Do the destructive images of wind and rain give a **tragic** dimension to the lives of the family members? Or does this poetic record of their activities (another example of a reclaiming of the past) testify to the enduring human spirit? The refrain in line six of each stanza (which is a feature the poem borrows from **ballad** form) certainly tends to point up the contrasts between past and present, order and destruction, happiness and loss. But in other respects, Hardy strives to moderate the potential **ironies** of the poem's juxtapositions. And in the final stanza the use of the verb 'ploughs', with its associations of cultivation and fertility, is a surprising way of describing the raindrops running down the tombstones. All these points will be addressed in further discussion of the poem in the Extended Commentaries.

T HE SHADOW ON THE STONE

This poem, which was first drafted in 1913, should be read in the light of the _Poems of 1912–13_ sequence. There, Hardy had, finally, managed to distance himself from his dead wife; here, he refuses to suppress the resurgence of his old affection for her

Walking by the 'Druid stone' which stands in the garden of Max Gate, his Dorchester home (and where Emma is said to have burnt his love letters), Hardy thinks that the shadow cast on it by a tree resembles that of Emma when she gardened nearby. It is as if the woman whose loss he had come to terms with is standing behind him, but he refuses to turn and extinguish the hope that her ghost might really be there as the old feelings are stirred in him.

Here Hardy poignantly rewrites the story of Orpheus, who went down into the underworld to bring back his dead wife Eurydice. The music of his lyre had won over the gods, who had decreed that he could return to the world of the living with her so long as he did not look back to see if she was following. At the last moment, however, overcome with longing for his wife, he glanced back, and she was lost to him forever. Unlike Orpheus, Hardy resists the temptation to look back. He does so not out of love, but because he fears that she is not there at all. Thus, as he leaves the 'glade' (like Orpheus returning from the underworld), doubt is present but he keeps open the possibility that Emma is indeed there. This is of course only a 'dream' (and the poem suppresses any supernatural explanation for the event) but it is very compelling nevertheless: the poem finally comprises a very human act of faith which challenges the realities of time and death.

Part of the appeal of the poem is its restrained, even tentative, tone as Hardy reflects on the situation. This derives partly from the sustained speech **rhythms**, and the sense that Hardy is confiding in the reader. Doubt and faith are kept in fine tension in this poem, most notably in the double negative 'Nay, I'll not unvision', where, with the use of the 'un'-compound he has coined, Hardy refuses to erase the possibility his heart longs for but which his head tells him is impossible. Hardy's paradoxical notion that inanimate rock carries traces of the human activities which have occurred in its vicinity can also be found in 'At Castle Boterel'.

'FOR LIFE I HAD NEVER CARED GREATLY'

Hardy meditates on his attitudes to life. After a characteristically sceptical opening, the ending of the poem is surprisingly optimistic

Hardy's early experiences had taught him to expect little from life. This was partly perhaps temperamental. Eventually, **alienation** proved to be marginally less appealing than a commitment to life. However, the old mood returned – until parting clouds revealed a star brightly shining in the sky and this vision gave Hardy a new resolve to carry on.

In characteristically reticent manner, Hardy says something in this poem about his refusal to be overwhelmed by pessimism – to succumb to the dead end of alienation – and his struggle to affirm human values in a universe apparently devoid of meaning. In later years, too, as part of his wish to trace the patterns of his own experience, he developed the view that his self-protective, reticent manner had played a part in shaping the predetermined course of his life – and crucially, the failure, through a breakdown of communication, of the relationship with Emma.

Here, however, the poem ends with uncharacteristic optimism. Notice, though, how the vision comes unbidden – life 'uncloaked a star' – and as much by chance as the 'peradventures', or hazards, encountered earlier. At the end of the poem Hardy finds himself once again journeying across a bleak landscape but now with new determination. The **metaphor** of life as a journey – a 'pilgrimage' – and indeed the **personification** of Life itself in the poem (not God, but strangely reminiscent of such a figure), disclose Hardy's attachment to the **imagery** and forms of a religious faith he has lost.

peradventures chance happenings
haply by chance

THE PITY OF IT

Hardy was appalled by the First World War: it shattered his lingering hopes that the world was slowly becoming a better place. This poem exploits the ironies of a conflict between peoples Hardy believed to be of the same race

Walking in deepest Dorset, Hardy says he has heard uses of an ancient **dialect** which resembles the language of the German adversaries. Using this as the basis for an assertion that the war is therefore between 'kin folk kin tongued', he says the Germans have been led astray by the selfishness of their leaders, men the poem roundly curses.

The poem is a **sonnet**: the octave sets out Hardy's evidence for kinship between the English and the Germans; the sestet delivers the curse through the mouth of the 'Heart crying'.

Interestingly, Hardy's contempt is not reserved for the German oligarchs ('gangs whose glory threats and slaughters are'), but is directed too at the forces of progress in **Victorian** England. In the first **stanza**, he tells us he walked 'afar / From rail-track': for Hardy, the railway, pushing into the Dorset countryside in a destructive reality, also assumed the status of a **symbol** for all those forces of homogenisation and centralisation, the products of an aggressive, middle-class, commercial civilisation, which were destroying older ways of life and eradicating the rural dialect.

This is an overtly political poem (modelled on William Wordsworth's political sonnets). The title is taken from Shakespeare's *Othello* (Act

IV Scene 1) when the protagonist, misled by Iago into thinking his wife Desdemona has been unfaithful, declares 'but yet the pity of it, Iago'. This literary **allusion** helps explain why Hardy uses a **personification**, a weeping Heart, to vent his spleen. Hardy is drawing a broad comparison between the plot of Shakespeare's **tragedy** and the case he presents here. The German people have been duped by their leaders, just as Othello is duped by Iago. As a consequence, German soldiers have gone to war with Britain, just as Othello murders Desdemona. Emilia, Iago's wife, finally tells Othello that Iago has tricked him. Saying her 'heart is full' – both for the innocent Desdemona and the gullible Othello – Emilia bitterly curses her husband's villainous lies. The words of the Heart in this poem echo those of Emilia.

The poem was widely criticised (by people Hardy thought had a vested interest in promoting the war) for its assertion of kinship between the English and the Germans. Hardy, however, replied that this was 'indisputable'.

'Thu bist', 'Er war' … 'Ich woll', 'Er sholl' the **dialect** survivals Hardy cites closely resemble the German language (in German, 'du bist', 'er war', 'ich will' and 'er soll' mean 'you are', 'he was', 'I want' and 'he should', respectively)

IN TIME OF 'THE BREAKING OF NATIONS'

Writing during the First World War, Hardy is keen to celebrate the unremarkable – but in some ways extraordinary – lives and work of ordinary people in contrast to that version of history which deals with great events

The man and the horse harrowing clods in the ploughed field; couch-grass being burnt off: the endless round of work on the land will go on year in, year out, while the hereditary rulers of Europe fall and are lost in history. Above all, the maid and her lover, who repeat the ancient story of romance, are seen to have more significance than the chronicles of war.

Hardy said that this poem developed from an idea he had during the Franco-Prussian War (in 1870) but was not written until the First World War was under way. 'Dynasties' (line 8) is a reference to the

Napoleonic Wars (1800–15) which ended at the Battle of Waterloo: Hardy's **epic** drama *The Dynasts*, which deals with this period, was published between 1903 and 1908. Hardy's point is that the figures mentioned in the poem will never appear in a conventional history book yet embody more human value and significance than the battles being fought in France. Dynasties will fall, but the 'maid and her wight', by marrying and having children, will make a greater contribution to the story of the human race.

Hardy was deeply suspicious of versions of history which were preoccupied with the exercise of power to the exclusion of the remarkable stories of ordinary men and women. In fact, many of his poems offer those stories (including his own) as a challenge to the processes of time. Here the 'maid and her wight' assume their roles in the timeless story of romance, in contrast to the strictly relative and specific events recorded in 'War's annals'. This privileging of (human) stories is also reinforced by the poem's form, particularly the echoes of folk-song in the **rhythms** and the **allusion** to the stories of **ballad** (the 'maid and her wight'). Moreover, the poem's apparent simplicity is deceptive. The numbered **stanzas** seem unconnected and the unity of the poem is perhaps only disclosed after several readings. The use of the phrase 'whispering by' to describe the arrival on the scene of the 'maid and her wight' is very effective: they are so anonymous, so unremarkable, but on reflection, so astonishing – which might also describe the method of the poem itself.

'The Breaking of Nations' a reference to the Old Testament: 'Thou art my battle axe and weapons of war: for with thee will I break in pieces the nations, and with thee will I destroy kingdoms' (Jeremiah 51:20). Jeremiah contrasts scenes of political strife and discord with scenes affirming the regenerative cycles of pastoral life

harrowing breaking up, levelling

couch-grass a weed burnt off at the end of the growing season

wight man; Hardy has chosen to use an archaic term (usually meaning 'human being' or 'person')

Afterwards

> At the age of seventy-seven (he was in fact to live for another ten years), Hardy writes his own epitaph – not, it has to be said, as the public figure (the author) but as a countryman who expects to be judged by his neighbours. He hopes he will be remembered for his curiosity, his keen eye for the beauties of nature and his concern for animals

In a series of **stanzas** Hardy wonders whether after his death, others will . remember him as a man who noticed the beauties of early summer, who was familiar with the flight of the nighthawk at dusk, who tried to protect animals from suffering, who had an eye for the mysteries of the heavens, and who noticed the way the sound of the church bells was carried on the breeze.

Here Hardy writes about his own death as if from beyond the grave. The poem in this sense confirms the **image** he had of himself after Emma's death as 'a dead man held on end' ('The Going'). But, just as in the poems about Emma, there is an attempt to bring the 'dead' person to life as Hardy not only talks about the things that mattered to him, but seeks to identify his uniqueness as an individual. The poem achieves this effectively, both through its slow, gentle **rhythms** which represent Hardy's self-effacing manner, and through the detailed images of nature in each stanza which confirm that he was indeed 'a man who used to notice such things'. These merit close attention not just because they are so vivid (Hardy's genius for the compound epithet is very evident here: see Language & Style) but because embedded in them too is a record of those moments when Hardy imagines himself passing from life to death – for example, the 'eyelid's soundless blink', which both describes the flight of the hawk and represents the moment of death. The poem concludes with Hardy envisaging his own funeral.

Indeed, the poem is quietly insistent on the passage of time. This is achieved in part by the repetition of 'when' in each stanza, which provides the context for Hardy's 'tremulous stay' on earth and inevitable but unremarkable death (he sees himself as slipping out of the back door of life). The sense of passing time is reinforced by the duration of a day, which is also the passage of the seasons, from a bright morning (in May) through dusk (autumn) and finally to night (winter). This is a convention of **elegy** but there is nothing routine about Hardy's use of it. There is even a suggestion that the process is completed, with Hardy being reabsorbed into the natural world and the return of spring in the last stanza. Notice how the 'outrollings' of the bell 'rise again'. There is no sense of a resurrection in religious terms here, but there certainly is a suggestion that Hardy can be 'resurrected' in the memories of those who knew him, and in the poem itself. This is another way in which Hardy attempts to show that human consciousness – here, surviving minds which bear the traces of memory of those who have gone – resists the passage of time. Hardy is so often labelled as a pessimist, but there are grounds for seeing this as a quietly optimistic poem.

postern back door
tremulous trembling

'AND THERE WAS A GREAT CALM'

This poem was written to mark the end of the First World War. As silence falls on the battlefields of Europe, Hardy answers those who lament the death and destruction of the previous four years by saying it was meant to be

During the war love and compassion were eclipsed. The domestic population grew more fearful. Hopes that the earth was becoming a better place to inhabit were dead – when suddenly the fighting stopped. The voices of those who had long wondered what purpose the carnage had served were again heard, but the forces which underwrite the events of the universe had completed their inevitable course.

The title is a reference to Matthew's Gospel (8:26) when Jesus rebukes the winds and the sea and a 'great calm' falls. Hardy uses this poem to reiterate his belief that the universe is governed by an 'iron Necessity', the power behind existence which he calls the 'Spirit of Irony' here and the 'Immanent Will' elsewhere (see 'The Convergence of the Twain' and the discussion of this in Themes).

Numbering himself among the 'bereft, and meek, and lowly', Hardy had hoped the world would become a better place as the goodwill of humankind began to inform the Will of the universe (Hardy's 'evolutionary meliorism'). But the First World War shattered this hope.

The effectiveness of the poem depends upon the sound and fury of the first five **stanzas**, compared with the silences (in part conveyed by so many negatives) of the final four. The scenes are described with telling detail. Hardy gives imaginative substance to the thoughts being worked out here by **personifying** the various abstractions he mentions (Care, Pity, etc.) – including the Spirit of Irony, which led some readers to believe, erroneously, that he believed in a malign God when in fact for Hardy the Immanent Will is always an unconscious force. Paradoxically, even after the guns have been silenced the Spirit of Pity can still only whisper its question (why was this suffering necessary?): by now, Hardy's hopes that war might be eradicated in the future have dissolved (see also ' "We Are Getting to the End" ').

thinned peoples by recruitment and slaughter, and (in Europe) the desertion of towns and villages

'Huns' a derogatory name for Germans

Sirius the brightest star in the sky and the chief star in the constellation Canis Major (also known as the Dog Star)

in good sooth truly

peradventures chance events

spray small branch or twig

weft-winged engines aeroplanes

Sɴᴏᴡ ɪɴ ᴛʜᴇ sᴜʙᴜʀʙs

It would be a mistake to read too much into this poem, to seek symbolic meanings. Its deeper significance, if any, lies in what it implies about the nature of poetry itself

The poem opens with a description of a snowfall in a suburban street and the way the scene is altered. A sparrow is almost buried when, alighting on a branch, it dislodges the snow; this sets off a further cascade.

A black cat tentatively and hopefully approaches a house door and the Hardys let it in.

> This is a clever poem which seeks to erase itself in the same way that the snow obliterates the suburban scene. Economic in style from the outset, the poem reduces itself to nothing. The **rhythms** of the poem convey what movement there is in the scene, but this is towards stillness as the falling snow eclipses the stirrings of life in the poem – the sparrow and the cat. The covering effects of the snow are represented in the poem's shape which, with appropriate irregularity emulating the swirling movement of the snow, occupies increasingly less space on the page – finally narrowing down to monosyllabic words, and the closing door. The page – and the street – are left in blank silence.
>
> The poem strives to give the illusion of **impersonality** and it is really only at the end that we become aware of an observer. After all, then, the reader is forced to consider the poem as an artefact, contrived by a human mind. We realise that the poem only exists because of the poet's consciousness, deploying language to organise the randomness of experience, selecting the detail and patterning it in the ways suggested above. It is this awareness of itself as a verbal construct as well as its minimalist style that have led some critics to see this poem as **modernist** – and specifically **imagist** – in its attempt to capture moments in time.
>
> **inurns** buries

DAYS TO RECOLLECT

> **This poem, written some thirteen years after Emma's death, returns to an old theme but without the anguish of earlier treatments. Indeed, it moves beyond its immediate subject to say something more general about the importance of memory**

Hardy affects to ask Emma if she remembers a walk they took together (in 1875). He recalls it vividly, but there is no response from her. So he asks if she recalls the day of her death, which changed everything for him.

As a measure of the time which has elapsed since the earliest days of his mourning for Emma (and the associated poems), the tone of the first **stanza** at least is striking. It seems that he now feels he can tease her for being dead ('You don't recall / That day in Fall?'). He has internalised her memory to the extent that he can take this kind of liberty. In fact, the juxtaposition of the earlier memory of the walk with the later memory, the day of her death, gives this familiarity a touching wryness. By the end of the poem the tone has modulated into something more plaintive, emphasised by the pauses in the last three lines.

The memories, as so often in Hardy's poetry, are vivid and complex. Here they are contrasted, and linked. Emma's dress stirs up the thistle-seeds. Her vitality is suggested by the way they follow her 'Like a comet's tail'. But this also hints at her mortality and is perhaps an omen of future unhappiness. When the rising seeds are compared to the 'ghosts ... of the recent dead' the **image** becomes prophetic and we are reminded that Emma and the incident survive only in the memory of the poet. In the second stanza Emma's acceptance in life of the 'gifts that Fortune bore, / Sharing, enduring, joys, hopes, fears!' harks back to those ambivalent 'Winged thistle-seeds' streaming behind her younger self. Hardy guards the memories of his wife, but they are a cause for self-reproach as well as fond recollection.

H<small>E NEVER EXPECTED MUCH</small>

On his eighty-sixth birthday Hardy reflects that life has turned out much as he expected. This poem stands as another justification of his pessimism

Even as a child, Hardy's expectations of life were minimal, and the passing years have confirmed this view. People respond to life in different ways – eagerly, serenely, contemptuously – but Hardy's perception that this is a world of cruelty and chance has enabled him to cope and survive.

Much of the appeal of this poem depends upon its wistful, meditative tone: it is indeed the voice of the old man reflecting on a lifetime. The tone is generated in large measure by the **stanza** pattern and the

refrain in the second line, and also by the sense of a quiet dialogue going on with another old person, in this case the 'World', the abstraction **personified** as so often in Hardy's poetry. At the end of his life, Hardy seems almost to view the world of time and chance ('neutral-tinted haps and such'), with which he has so often struggled, as a friend and mentor.

The poem constitutes a distilling of that self-protective detachment from life which has informed so many of the earlier poems. One might compare it with ' "For Life I Had Never Cared Greatly" ', for example. But that poem hints at what is omitted here: that Hardy elsewhere often fights back, struggles against feelings of **alienation**, in order to overcome the indifference of time (by reclaiming the past) and space (by putting human meaning back into the landscape). It could be argued that this poem represents the equanimity of old age. Or perhaps the effect of the 'Well ...' which opens the poem, in conjunction with the somewhat listless **refrain**, is to suggest resignation – or simply weariness.

leaze (dialect) pasture

STANDING BY THE MANTELPIECE

The words are spoken by Horace Mosley Moule, a friend of Hardy's who encouraged his writing career. Moule committed suicide in his rooms at Queen's College, Cambridge on 21 September 1873

Moule notices that the burning candle is producing a shroud-shaped column of wax, and touches it, knowing the superstition that this phenomenon forecasts a death. He is in a suicidal mood and he bitterly reproaches an (unidentified) woman for breaking off their engagement (in circumstances which are not clear). Finally, he touches the shroud of wax on the candle again.

The circularity of this poem – returning to where it starts with the reference to the shroud of candle-wax – is its most effective feature. When Moule claims for himself the death foretold by touching the wax the second time, it is more disturbing in the light of the disclosure of his black mood in the interim. The folk tradition gains a sinister force as it assumes a reality in Moule's experience. Perhaps, too, the circularity reinforces Moule's hopeless state of mind and the inevitable way 'finality / Closes around'.

But this early poem (published posthumously) is in some respects rather disappointing after all. This is largely because of its portentous Shakespearean echoes: the superstition, the **melodramatic** gesture, the **allusions** (for example, Iago's refusal to speak again at the end of *Othello*, and Hamlet's 'The rest is silence') and the **iambic pentameters**. Hardy was reading the Shakespearean **tragedies** when he wrote this and their influence is clear. The consequence – so uncharacteristic of Hardy's poems about the dead – is that we learn hardly anything about Moule himself.

drape a hanging (usually fabric) which covers something in folds: shroud

'WE ARE GETTING TO THE END'

This is a late, dark poem in which Hardy expresses the failure of his hopes for the human race. It is characteristic of his attitude after the First World War and suggests that he could see the second one coming

Hardy says that he can no longer envision the betterment of the human race. He now feels that the expression of such hopes for freedom are like the song of a caged bird – self-deluding and forever doomed to disappointment. And he knows that nations will not hesitate to repeat the destruction of neighbouring countries when incited to do so.

The tight form of a **sonnet** is very appropriate for this deeply sceptical poem, which argues that freedom ('pleasuring') is actually an illusion when the real conditions of existence, the forces of the universe which operate in both personal and public life, are in fact those of imprisonment. The poet, like the bird, may 'sing' his hopes but both are caged – indeed, both know full well that their efforts will be ineffectual. This seems to be Hardy's bleak final judgement on his poetic objectives, the struggle to reassert human value and meaning ('visioning') in the face of a material universe of space and time.

Finally, Hardy bitterly predicts that nations will embark on future wars when 'tickled mad by some demonic force'. 'Yes' he says, with scornful finality, 'We are getting to the end of dreams!'

By now Hardy's 'evolutionary meliorism', the belief that the world could be made better by human effort, has faded into despair. At one time he had even thought that this process might inform the forces of the universe, which he elsewhere calls the 'Immanent Will' (see Themes). But in this poem a sense of the 'iron Necessity' at work in the affairs of individuals and societies (which curtails individual freedom and drives nations to war) seems to be solidly back in place. Nevertheless, Hardy does voice his exasperation with the human race in the sestet (the last six lines) – though without any of the conceptual sophistication of 'The Convergence of the Twain', where it seems that the Immanent Will can be provoked into malignity by human vanity. Here Hardy sounds more like a splenetic old man and the poetry fails. After the First World War, nations never called up the cavalry when they went to war and the use of 'horse' seems to depend simply on the need for a rhyme with 'force'. And the poem descends into **bathos** when Hardy claims that modern nations go to war when 'tickled mad by some demonic force'.

latticed hearse the cage, however pretty, will deliver the bird to the grave – which it therefore prefigures
foot and horse infantry and cavalry
warely cautiously

HE RESOLVES TO SAY NO MORE

Hardy intended this poem to mark the closure of his poetic career and it was actually published after his death

Hardy suggests that he has had an apocalyptic vision of the future, but he resolves to take it with him to the grave. Human beings already have more than enough to cope with. Even assuming it will become possible to see into the future, Hardy will not reveal what he has seen. Nor will he speak out simply because his foresight goes beyond the limitations of others.

Hardy assembles the reasons why he will say no more. The **rhetorical** trick Hardy employs here is to seem to withhold meaning while nevertheless putting forward his ideas, and the whole poem exhibits this double movement of deferral and disclosure. Following the First World War, which dismayed him so much and dashed his hopes for 'evolutionary meliorism' (see Themes), Hardy recognises that humanity can do without more cause of suffering. But he tantalisingly suggests, with the reference to the 'charnel-eyed / Pale Horse' of Death, that there is worse to come. With the benefit of hindsight, this seems to be a prediction of the Second World War.

Hardy's reflections on 'Time' in **stanzas** three and four develop the same impatience with the human race he evinced in the previous poem (' "We Are Getting to the End" '). It is **ironic**, he suggests, that while some wise men predict the possibility of seeing into the future, the majority of the human race seems to be moving backwards in time. Hardy thought that the barbarism of the First World War had demonstrated this. Thus he can say that his vision exceeds the 'blinkered sight of souls in bond', where Hardy revives the **image** of imprisonment used in the previous poem. But again, the cause of this is not the forces of the universe, but human beings' refusal to grasp the 'truth' which would make them 'free'. As a consequence, Hardy's resolution to say no more actually becomes sardonically eloquent: the human race doesn't deserve the poet's 'vision'.

charnel deathly (a charnel house is a place where corpses or bones are deposited)
Magians wise men

PART THREE

CRITICAL APPROACHES

THEMES

Victorians saw themselves as victims of time – and Thomas Hardy, whose intellectually formative years were in the 1860s and 1870s, was no exception. The passage of time is the central theme in his poetry: he believed that it was the source of all the unhappiness in the world. A related theme concerns his perception of the indifference of the enduring landscape to the short lives of human beings. Hardy thought that humanity was dwarfed by the forces of the universe and, like many others in the latter years of the nineteenth century, he felt a deep sense of **alienation** and personal insignificance.

Certainly in Hardy's view, human beings could expect little from life. To be conscious was, for Hardy, to feel pain, to see your hopes dashed, to lose loved ones, to suffer the depredations of time. Life was a downward spiral towards an inevitable conclusion. Hardy saw this as the 'web of fate' in which individual human lives (and indeed whole societies, for this was a view of history too) were enmeshed. But this is not all we find in Hardy's work, and it is vital to understand that the pessimism is offset by resistance. In many of his most memorable poems (for example, 'At Castle Boterel', 'During Wind and Rain' and 'Afterwards') the same consciousness that feels pain also struggles against the meaninglessness of space and time, and seeks to reassert the essentially human against the forces of the universe.

What were the sources of Hardy's pessimism? Part of the problem was Victorian middle-class society itself and its obsession with 'Progress'. It seemed to Hardy that such an **ideology** only intensified individuals' vulnerability to the destructiveness of time. He could not accept the Victorian notion of divine Providence, a God-given plan for the world which worked towards good. But for many of his contemporaries in the middle years of the century, the march of time and the development of Victorian middle-class civilisation seemed to be running reassuringly in parallel. Hardy didn't share this optimism (see Historical Background for further discussion). For him, there was a depressing inevitability about the way middle-class society was making inroads into all areas of life and it seemed to bring with it a growing sense of loneliness and emptiness. Hardy often used the phenomenon of the railway (reaching into Dorset when he was a young man and dislocating long-established communities and customs) as a **symbol** for this process – running like time itself, inexorably onwards and crushing everything human in its path.

The complacency of the Victorian middle classes was shattered by the publication of Charles Darwin's *On the Origin of Species by Means of Natural Selection: or, The Preservation of Favoured Races in the Struggle for Life* in 1859. Ideas about evolution had been around for many years. The difference in Darwin's case was that he developed a powerful theory to explain it: in the competitive struggle for existence, chance mutations could confer particular advantages on some creatures which might then develop into new species. The randomness of the process of natural selection made it difficult to believe that history had a design and purpose. Middle-class ideology and Darwinism were allied in Hardy's view: one had drained reality of meaning by putting the doctrine of 'Progress' before human relationships; the other had generated a view of the environment which had reduced human beings to insignificant victims.

But Hardy doesn't submit: within some of his best poems there is considerable resistance in consciousness to these determining factors. Firstly, acts of memory – attempts to reclaim the past – strive to resist the processes of change and loss, and, related to this, visionary insight seeks to imbue the indifferent landscape with human meaning. Secondly, the search both in the private and public spheres to find patterns in the flux of experience indicates a very human wish to fend off feelings of meaninglessness.

RECLAIMING THE PAST

Why is Hardy so keen to recover the past in poem after poem? It is not because, as has sometimes been claimed, he was incapable of living in the present – although he did recognise that people, himself included, found it increasingly difficult, in the words of the Roman poet Horace, to 'seize the day' (*carpe diem*), an exhortation to make the best use of time before it is too late. This was one consequence of the **alienated** consciousness. Nor is it simply because of an assumption that the past must be better – although in many poems the past is **ironically** counterpointed with an unhappy present.

Hardy's attempts to reclaim the past in memory are in fact a way of regenerating the present by reaffirming those human values which he considered to have been more active in the rural world he grew up in half a century before – a world then largely untouched by middle-class **ideology** and Darwinian science. Hardy felt there was an urgent need to put humanity back into history and the landscape, and in fact the effort to do so shows him struggling with the alienated tendencies of his own outlook – and many poems (such as 'The Darkling Thrush', 'In Tenebris I', 'After a Journey' and 'Places') demonstrate that this was no easy task.

Feelings of alienation account for Hardy's characteristic stance of lonely retrospection. The voice we hear is again and again that of an old man, whose life is to all intents and purposes over, looking back on his past. In 'The Going' he describes himself as a 'dead man held on end' – a man who has lived beyond his time, surviving both friends and family. However, this does not preclude (and in some cases it even prompts) visions which defy the materiality of time and space – visions of a history which privileges human relationships or landscapes imbued with human meanings. And, as one might expect from a writer who persistently plunders memory and the past for his subjects, Hardy's poems are haunted by the ghosts of the dead – in particular his wife Emma, for whom he wrote the famous sequence of **elegies** which make up the *Poems of 1912–13*. But Hardy's recovery of the dead is usually intended to provide lessons for the living.

Writing from the detached stance of a 'dead man held on end' also shapes Hardy's characteristically reticent manner, his unwillingness to give too much away even when he is writing about himself and his own life. This is partly a means of self-protection, for Hardy was deeply affected by the controversy generated by the last novels (it is significant that he had doubts about publishing the *Poems of 1912–13* at all). But it is a reticence which is paradoxically eloquent, for in poems like 'The Self-Unseeing' and 'During Wind and Rain' the very lack of specificity gives the reclamation of the past a universal human relevance and force.

PATTERNS

The habit of retrospection gives rise to the **ironic** counterpointing of past and present which is a recurrent structural feature of Hardy's poetry (see, for example, 'The Five Students', 'During Wind and Rain', 'Afterwards' and many of the *Poems of 1912–13*). But in fact Hardy was always keen to discover and highlight antithetical patterns in experience, and thematic comparison/contrast can be found in many of his poems – for example, iceberg and ship (in 'The Convergence of the Twain'), Dorset and South Africa (in 'Drummer Hodge'), the human individual and the landscape (in 'The Darkling Thrush'), hills and lowlands (in 'Wessex Heights'). These antitheses, which are evident in the detail (of **rhyme, metre** and **stanza**) as well as in the overall structure, are the source of meaning and feeling in many poems. Further discussion can be found in the Commentaries of the poems mentioned, and in Techniques on Versification.

Hardy also has a desire to find patterns in his own personal story – and of course retrospection facilitates this. In effect, the main subject of his poetry is Hardy himself and many poems attempt to recount the narrative of his life. Central to this narrative is Emma's death, which prompted the uncomfortable recognition that his love for her was the keystone of his story (this recognition provides the motive behind the *Poems of 1912–13*). The search for patterns in his own life – and in the wider human experience – represents further evidence of Hardy's resistance to the meaninglessness of time and space, and in particular the web of fate which he believed circumscribed all human activity. Indeed, the attempt to *understand* the workings of fate in both the personal and public dimensions was itself a form of that resistance.

There is something very paradoxical about Hardy's attempts to locate patterns: if the universe is meaningless, how could it evince patterns? The answer to this lies in Hardy's reaction to his loss of faith. When Hardy's Christian belief dissolved around 1865 he, like many Victorians in the same position, felt an acute sense of loss. While he rejected the notion of a divine Providence, the impulse to believe in some force which shaped experience still remained active. Hardy emphasised that this force was indifferent and unconscious and he called it various names including the 'Immanent Will' (see, for example, 'The Convergence of the Twain'). By this he meant the abstract principle (it needs to be remembered that he understood this **metaphorically**) which underwrites all personal and public events, the web of fate which circumscribes all human life.

But while Hardy seems to have accepted that the universe was governed by an 'iron Necessity', he continued to speculate in his poetry about the part that humans could play in shaping their own destiny – for better or worse. He often denied that he was a pessimist, and preferred to be seen as an 'evolutionary meliorist', that is, he tried to believe that the world could be improved by collective human effort. He also hoped that this might influence the workings of the Immanent Will for the better. However, the First World War shattered these hopes. By the end of his life Hardy's view that the Immanent Will was utterly indifferent to human life had hardened and he even wondered if it could be tipped into malignity by human folly.

POEMS OF 1912–13

Emma Hardy died suddenly at Max Gate, the Hardys' Dorchester home, on 27 November 1912. She was seventy-two years old, the same age as her husband. Relations between them had not been good for many years – a process accelerated by the publication of *Jude the Obscure*, to which the evangelical Emma objected for both its religious unorthodoxy and its bitter portrayal of marriage. However, her death shocked Hardy greatly. He was consumed with guilt for the way he had treated her but also experienced an intense revival of the love he had felt for her in the early years of their relationship. In March 1913 he undertook a pilgrimage to Cornwall and the locations of their courtship exactly forty-three years before.

The outcome of these events was a sequence of moving poems of memory and grief – even of atonement. For these reasons it is perhaps understandable why Hardy hesitated over the publication of these very personal poems, although they include some of his finest work. The *Poems of 1912–13* are **elegies** but in various ways they challenge the traditional elegiac form – and, indeed, are unusual in a more general sense in that the subject is the poet's wife.

Previous elegies, such as Tennyson's *In Memoriam*, had followed a conventional pattern which paralleled the normal processes of mourning and coming to terms with the loss of a loved one: shock at the person's death, followed by despair, resignation and finally reconciliation. The *Poems of 1912–13* reflect this pattern but with significant variations. The early poems ('The Going', 'Your Last Drive', 'The Walk' and 'Without Ceremony') do follow convention in that they record Hardy's shock at Emma's death. In common with the elegiac tradition there is a refusal to believe she has died; grief alternates with defiance and even irritation (we sense that Hardy is almost asking 'how could you do this to me?'). These poems all deal with the older Emma at Max Gate and with the scene of her death, and show Hardy making initial efforts to come to terms with it. Often the tone modulates into despair.

In conventional elegiac sequences the next stages of the **cycle** show the distancing of the poet from the dead loved one (resignation), the placing of her into consolatory natural processes and finally her integration into memory (reconciliation). 'Rain on a Grave', ' "I Found Her Out There"' and 'Lament' are the most conventional elegies in the sequence. They seem to be written without much conviction partly because it goes against the grain for Hardy, with his profound sense of an indifferent universe, to sentimentalise nature as a site where Emma can be reborn in spirit, and partly because Hardy's grief (with its attendant guilt) is too complex to be accommodated by the traditional framework and **motifs**. Indeed, any stirrings of recovery prove to be short-lived. 'The Voice' is undoubtedly the bleakest poem of the sequence and it marks a return to despair. Conventional elegiacs have therefore largely failed Hardy and it is in light of this that he makes the decision (in 'A Dream or No') to go to Cornwall and the scenes of his courtship of Emma.

These more conventional elegies do, however, play a part in the progress of Hardy's mourning: they erase the old Emma (in 'His Visitor' he leaves Max Gate for the last time) and, by distancing Hardy from his loss, they confirm that he is becoming more resigned to her death. The outcome of this is the creation of an ideal **image** of Emma – young, vital and warm – in the core poems of the sequence set in Cornwall: 'After a Journey', 'Beeny Cliff' and 'At Castle Boterel'. Thus Hardy achieves his own form of reconciliation (and in 'A Death-Day Recalled' he specifically rejects conventional elegiacs) – one which is complex and ambivalent.

Indeed, there has been much critical debate over the nature of the reconciliation which Hardy achieves in these final poems. Some critics see them as demonstrating how love can conquer time. Perhaps it is safer to say that they are rather more tentative, that they are poems which reclaim those idyllic moments from the past but also record a profound sense of the loss wrought by change and death. And the measure of this ambivalence is the extent to which Hardy rejects the forms of the traditional elegy.

These poems are, as so often in Hardy's work, retrospective: they see a happy past from the perspective of a grieving present. But it must be remembered that here the present is doubly unhappy. Love had died between the Hardys before Emma's actual death, as the poems themselves make clear. Thus the anguish of Hardy's bereavement was intense and his elegies are unconventional in that they are guilt-ridden and withhold consolation. This is why the view that love conquers time in these poems is unsatisfactory: Hardy's poetic resurrection of the youthful Emma during that idyllic courtship is qualified by a parallel recognition that she is dead, that things ended badly between them and that nothing can now be changed. 'After a Journey' ends in bitterness, and the final **stanza** of 'At Castle Boterel' sees the aged Hardy bidding a sad farewell to Emma's ghost.

Finally, do these guilty feelings explain why, after three attempts to give Emma a voice in the sequence ('The Haunter', 'The Voice' and 'His Visitor'), Hardy settles for vision? The poetic effort to restore meaning to the landscape by envisioning Emma's presence in it is a perfectly valid one, as it reaffirms the human in a material universe of time and space (and it is no easy task here as the enduring, formidable landscapes of these Cornwall poems make clear). But perhaps the ghost's silence is an **ironic** recognition of the failure of communication in their marriage which caused the grieving Hardy so much pain.

TECHNIQUES

Thomas Hardy's poetry is characterised by a tension, even a contradiction, between underlying form (the search for patterns) and surface roughness (the recognition of the disorderly nature of experience). The poems are highly crafted, employing complex **verse forms**, but also evincing idiosyncrasies of **diction** and **syntax** and the wilful disruption of **metrical** patterns.

Hardy responded to the charge of crudeness to which these features sometimes gave rise by claiming an affinity between his poetic practice and Gothic art (represented, for example, by the great European cathedrals) which, he said, also recognised the need for fundamental structure but valued spontaneity and freedom as well. It must be remembered that Hardy was initially trained as an architect at a time when the Gothic revival in church building and restoration was in full swing. In his autobiography Hardy claimed, in comments which owe a clear debt to John Ruskin's chapter 'The Nature of Gothic' in the great architectural study *The Stones of Venice* (1853), that his critics had missed the point:

> That the author loved the art of concealing art was undiscerned. For instance, as to rhythm. Years earlier he had decided that too regular a beat was bad art. He had fortified himself in his opinion by thinking of the analogy of architecture, between which art and that of poetry he had discovered, to use his own words, that there existed a close and curious parallel, both arts, unlike some others, having to carry a rational content inside their artistic form. He knew that in architecture cunning irregularity is of enormous worth, and it is obvious that he carried on into his verse, perhaps in part unconsciously, the Gothic art-principle in which he had been trained – the principle of spontaneity found in mouldings, tracery, and such like – resulting in the 'unforeseen' (as it has been called) character of his metres and stanzas, that of stress rather than of syllable, poetic texture rather than poetic veneer; the latter kind of thing, under the name of 'constructed ornament', being what he, in common with every Gothic student, had been taught to avoid like the plague.

Hardy sought freshness and vitality in his poetry ('the principle of spontaneity') – and was always prepared to break the rules of poetic decorum in general, and those of **metre, diction** and **syntax** in particular ('cunning irregularity'). But this is not to say that he did not continue to believe in *underlying* form or pattern (the poem's 'rational content').

Hardy's views were informed by a fundamental conviction that what poetry said (its 'poetic texture') was much more important than the way it said it (its 'poetic veneer'). In other words, a successful poem – one that properly engaged with life – was one which scrupulously sought to express the 'truth' even if it had some rough edges. Language, particularly written text, which was too polished was liable to become lifeless (and this also explains why Hardy continually strove to create the impression of voices in his poetry). For while there is a strong desire in Hardy's verse to disclose the patterns which might resist the meaninglessness of existence (see Themes), there is also a vivid sense of the randomness of lived experience. This is the source of the thematic ambivalence which characterises so many poems (see, for example, 'During Wind and Rain').

In rejecting 'poetic veneer' – 'the art', as he describes it elsewhere, 'of saying nothing in mellifluous syllables' – and instead deliberately cultivating an 'irregularity' in his poetry, Hardy was emphatically rejecting what he saw as the 'smoothness' of his Victorian predecessors. Writing to Edmund Gosse, Hardy declared: 'For as long as I can remember my instinctive feeling has been to avoid the jewelled line in poetry as being effeminate.' This has often been taken to be an attack on Tennyson. But while he urgently wanted to forge his own style, Hardy in fact admired Tennyson – and sometimes the reader can hear the older poet's influence (as in the wonderful opening line of 'Beeny Cliff': 'O the opal and the sapphire of that wandering western sea'). Hardy's real target was F.T. Palgrave's *Golden Treasury* (1861), an influential, best-selling **anthology** (compiled, it must be said, with Tennyson's assistance) of Victorian poetry. Hardy felt that this volume, with its emphasis on poetry as escapism and its high style removed from everyday language, had disastrously shaped the poetic expectations of a generation.

As detailed in the Commentaries, fundamental to Hardy's poetic aspirations is a wish to revitalise the present by recovering the past: together, art and memory can challenge the onward march of time. But memory, and therefore poetic truth, will be betrayed if the representation of the events recalled is falsified by sentimentality, idealisation or, simply, an overly punctilious treatment. Hardy always endeavoured to capture the truth of the experience he was relating, even if that meant disregarding the niceties of poetry and shocking the reader (indeed, Hardy felt he could be even more outspoken in his poetry than he had been in his novels). When memory is the only antidote to the depredations of time, then accuracy is vital: tidy things up, Hardy felt, and time will always win.

LANGUAGE & STYLE

In a generally enthusiastic lecture on Hardy's poetry delivered in 1951, Cecil Day-Lewis (who was Poet Laureate from 1968 to 1972) found fault with the first line of 'Afterwards' – 'When the Present has latched its postern behind my tremulous stay' – because of its odd mixture of the poetic, the archaic and the Latinate, and complained that it was an extraordinarily long-winded way of saying 'when I am dead'. This is a mild (and in fact affectionate) instance of the kind of adverse comment that

Hardy's language and style have regularly attracted. His choice of words, for instance, demonstrates a lively eclecticism ranging across – and often mixing – the academic and the **colloquial**, the rare and the familiar, the high-flown and the everyday. Hardy has a penchant, too, for the coining of new words and compounds. Moreover, the **syntax** in some poems occasionally evinces the same kind of eccentricity found in the **diction**: Hardy regularly employs complex and untidy sentences which can be very confusing, or frustrating, for the reader.

Commenting on Hardy's diction, F.R. Leavis (in an article entitled 'Hardy the Poet' which first appeared in *Southern Review* 6, 1940, pp. 87–98, reprinted in *F.R. Leavis: The Critic as Anti-Philosopher*, ed. G. Singh, Chatto & Windus, 1982, p. 99) expressed an academic, and distinctly patronising, view:

> If one says that he seems to have no sensitiveness for words, one recognises at the same time that he has made a style out of stylelessness. There is something extremely personal about the gauche, unshrinking mismarriages – group-mismarriages – of his diction, in which, with naif aplomb, he takes as they come the romantic-poetical, the prosaic banal, the stilted literary, the colloquial, the archaistic, the erudite, the technical, the dialect word, the brand-new Hardy coinage.

The charge of insensitivity and ignorance, coming from a critic of Leavis's stature, was very influential but is nevertheless unfair. In part, the odd juxtapositions of diction, and (sometimes) awkward word coinages, can be seen as further manifestations of the 'Gothic art-principle' described above. But in large measure, too, Hardy's diction reflects the particular circumstances of his career: a largely self-educated poet, born the son of a rural tradesman, he was outside the literary mainstream and did not subscribe to any centralised orthodoxy of what constituted a language appropriate for poetry.

So although Hardy often uses some very odd words such as 'scath' ('In Tenebris I'), 'continuator' ('Wessex Heights') and 'lours' ('After a Journey'), presses parts of speech into new roles ('obscure' is used as a noun in 'murked obscure' in 'Near Lanivet', for instance), and regularly draws on dialect (movingly in 'The Oxen'), the biggest problem for the literary purists is his tendency to mix the familiar with literary diction. An example of this is provided in the first stanza of 'The Darkling Thrush':

> I leant upon a coppice gate
>> When Frost was spectre-gray,
> And Winter's dregs made desolate
>> The weakening eye of day.

This has a self-consciously poetic style: the use of the word 'coppice'; the compound epithet 'spectre-gray', which describes the frost (a grey ghost); the implicit **metaphor** in 'the weakening eye of day', which suggests how the sun is diminished by the poor light and the cold weather. But in the midst of all this Hardy uses the homely word 'dregs', which brings to mind tea leaves at the bottom of an empty cup! However, in the context of the poem as a whole, with its suggestions of how life has been drained from the poet, his fellow human beings and the landscape – in contrast to the thrush's vigorous song – the word seems perfectly placed to evoke the sombre mood which opens the poem and which is never quite dispelled.

Hardy's word coinages are often rough but meant to revitalise more familiar words and expressions. His particular talent is for the use of compound epithets, a technique he learnt from his poetic mentor, William Barnes. They are particularly effective when Hardy turns a keen countryman's eye to the beauties of nature, for example in 'Afterwards' ('Delicate-filmed as new-spun silk'; 'wind-warped upland thorn'; 'full-starred heavens') and 'The Five Students' ('The sun grows passionate-eyed'; 'The home-bound foot-folk wrap their snow-flaked heads'). Hardy also had a talent for coining derivatives, usually with prefixes such as up-, out-, over-, in-, en- and un-, for example: 'bedrenches' ('At Castle Boterel'); 'outleant' ('The Darkling Thrush'); 'unvision' ('The Shadow on the Stone'); 'undistrest' (' "I Look Into My Glass" '); 'uncoffined' ('Drummer Hodge'); 'unhope' ('In Tenebris I'); 'inurns' ('Snow in the Suburbs'). Occasionally, a new word is generated by the use of a suffix, or in the case of 'wistlessness' ('The Voice'), two suffixes – a coinage which F.R. Leavis found to be 'a characteristic eccentricity of invention' (*New Bearings in English Poetry*, Chatto & Windus, 1961, p. 60). In all these cases, however, a sympathetic reading of the poem in which the words appear can justify their use in the particular context.

Sometimes it is not a question of a new coinage but the employment of the exact – and sometimes surprising – word where, again, the context confirms its appositeness. In 'Beeny Cliff', for example, the use of the word 'chasmal' (the adjective derived from the noun 'chasm') is not a coinage, but its use is sufficiently rare to give it the appearance of one. Similarly, in the same poem, the verb 'bulks', although a perfectly standard usage, sounds odd because it is usually coupled with 'large'. Here, these words effectively denote, after the poem's opening lyrical recollections, the poet's change of mood as he returns to present reality.

In a few cases Hardy's critics are perhaps justified, and his employment of unusual words can be seen to have a more utilitarian provenance. For example, the use of the archaic 'Christés' (Christ's) in 'Channel Firing' seems to have no other function than to complete the line's **metric** form. Equally, the use of 'alway' in 'He Resolves to Say No More' would seem to have rather more to do with completing the **triple rhyme** with which the first **stanza** ends than evoking a particular meaning.

Hardy's occasionally odd **syntax** is often the product of a desire to register nuances of situation or emotion rather than clumsiness. In 'Neutral Tones', for instance, the awkwardness in the second and third stanzas is a matter of grammar and gives the impression of a mind struggling to understand its experience – and evincing such strong emotions just beneath the poem's surface. The first stanza of 'Without Ceremony' attracted much negative criticism from contemporary reviewers who maintained it was 'unpoetic'. Here Hardy says that he 'inferred' Emma's sudden departures from home while alive to be the result of her capricious nature. 'Inferred' is delayed to the end of the stanza, which causes much of the syntactical problem, and raises the further difficulty that it seems to be there simply to rhyme with 'word'. But Emma's death has prompted him to wonder whether his inference was wrong (there were other reasons – including the wish to escape from his hostility – that prompted her behaviour) and the use of the word, and its postponement in the sentence, suggests something of his painful awakening. Sometimes, the syntactical oddity derives from a wish for economy of expression. In 'The Going', for example, the **couplet** 'Where I could not follow / With wing of swallow' should properly be 'As with the wing of a swallow'. On such occasions, Hardy risks the general accusation of obscurity, and more specifically the charge that he has mangled the language to make it fit the poem's metrical pattern.

VERSIFICATION

Hardy was fascinated by **prosody** and his poems employ an enormous variety of **metrical** styles and **verse forms**. These range from the sophisticated to the simple and indicate a continuing willingness to experiment with the raw materials of his craft. The *Poems of 1912–13* are representative in this respect: each has its own distinctive verse form and all display a range of metrical, **rhyming** and other symmetrical effects. But while Hardy uses a greater number of distinctive **stanza** forms than any other English poet, few are totally original ('After a Journey' and 'The Wind's Prophecy' can probably be numbered among the exceptions). Hardy was a poetic innovator, not a radical, and his experiments were based on a sense of continuity: he continued to favour traditional prosody – demonstrating a particular liking for **ballad** and hymn metres, for instance – and disliked **free verse**. There is no doubt, however, that his experimentation made a significant contribution to the subsequent development of English poetry.

Hardy's preference for the traditional forms is nowhere more evident than in his recurrent use of the ballad stanza (also known as the short hymn stanza or common measure; see also Ballad Form below). This comprises rhymed **iambic quatrains** – abab – with **tetrameter** a-lines and **trimeter** b-lines. In 'The Oxen' this form serves to enhance the nostalgia for the old days – and undergoes some variation in the third and fourth stanzas to suggest, even at the metrical level, how times have changed. Sometimes Hardy modifies the ballad stanza to suit his own purposes. At first glance, 'The Darkling Thrush' appears to use an original eight-line stanza, but a closer look shows that it actually comprises two ballad stanzas joined together. The emergence of a new form out of the vestiges of the old perhaps underlines the poem's modern scepticism, which finds older, more reassuring beliefs increasingly untenable and therefore cannot quite see the thrush as a source of 'Hope' after all.

Elsewhere Hardy uses more sophisticated traditional stanza forms to achieve specific effects. 'We Are Getting to the End', for example, is a **Petrarchan sonnet**. The sonnet is in some ways the most fixed of forms: its use is singularly apt here, as Hardy argues that human freedom is illusory. For 'Standing by the Mantelpiece', an epitaph for his dead friend Horace Moule, Hardy employs the traditional **elegiac** stanza (iambic **pentameters** rhymed abab). In '"When I Set Out for Lyonnesse"' Hardy adopts the traditional form of the **rondeau**. The first two lines of each stanza come round again and convey the young Hardy's excitement following his first meeting with Emma.

On occasion Hardy's poetry is more obviously experimental – most notably, perhaps, in his creation of irregular stanzas comprising lines of varying metrical lengths. In 'The Five Students' there are five separate line types. In each stanza the pattern followed is: **tetrameter, trimeter, pentameter**, a second trimeter, **hexameter** and **dimeter**, all mainly iambic and rhymed ababcc. The effect is to reinforce the antithetical nature of the poem, the onward march of life punctuated by the arrest of death, and narrowing to the single survivor (the poet), whose own days are numbered. Elsewhere the different line lengths work together to give the poem a shape on the page which is relevant to its subject or theme. The most striking example of this is 'The Convergence of the Twain', with its three rhyming (mostly iambic) lines (two dimeters and one hexameter) which suggest the image of a ship lying low in the water. In 'Snow in the Suburbs' the variety of line lengths emulates the swirling snow, and the poem finally erases itself – as the snow has covered the street – by narrowing to a dimeter line.

Hardy continued to believe that every poem should have a basic 'verse skeleton' but that it need not conform strictly to this: as long as the underlying pattern was recognised, the poem could depart from it to gain certain effects. For Hardy, this meant above all capturing the spontaneous rhythms of speech – not just in **dramatic monologues**, such as 'Standing by the Mantelpiece', but also in a more general attempt to emulate a consciousness (usually his own) striving to rescue some human meaning from a universe of time and change ('At Castle Boterel', for example) or reflecting on his experience ('The Shadow on the Stone', for instance, has the feel of a private meditation which the reader 'overhears').

Hardy's poetry therefore shows a recurring willingness to disrupt the underlying metrical patterns. In the first stanza of 'After a Journey', for example, the opening line suggests the basic metre is going to be iambic pentameter but it is quite impossible to sustain this reading, as the **stresses** (four to a line, with the exception of line seven) cut across the basic pattern. This is a result of the **syntax**, the strong **caesurae** in some lines, the frequent **anapaests** and the **feminine rhymes** – and it effectively confirms that the poet is indeed 'lonely, lost' as he revisits the sites of his courtship forty-three years before. But what seems strikingly effective to readers nearly a century later seemed less so to many of Hardy's first readers. His experiments, and particularly the disruption of metrical patterns, were widely criticised: many of Hardy's contemporaries were not yet ready for the variations of stress in lines of poetry which were to become normal in the **free verse** of the twentieth century.

A more serious charge, which continued into the twentieth century, was that Hardy sometimes forces his meanings into 'verse skeletons' which are not always appropriate for the mood of the poems. Donald Davie (in *Thomas Hardy and British Poetry*, Routledge & Kegan Paul, 1973) claims that this is the case with 'The Going'. Controversially, Davie, who describes Hardy as the 'laureate of engineering' (that is, a meticulous poetic craftsman who in this respect can be seen, paradoxically, as the product of nineteenth-century mechanisation), finds the poem to be overly symmetrical in ways which 'obstruct' the developing emotion. Davie writes that what we find is 'the imperious verbal engineer still, even here, thwarting the true and truly suffering poet' (p. 59). Elsewhere, however, Davie – who is actually a sympathetic and admiring critic of Hardy – concedes that Hardy's knowledge of metrical form works extremely well in a poem like 'The Convergence of the Twain'.

Hardy nearly always uses **rhyme**, often deploying elaborate schemes, for example in 'The Phantom Horsewoman', where the pattern employed (abcbcbcaa) is an attempt, together with certain **metrical** features, to echo in rhyme the ebb and flow of the tide with which the ghostly Emma is identified. Hardy favoured repeated rhymes as the foundation for stanzas – a characteristic which gives many poems a **ballad**-like feel, and the resulting sense that they deliver human truths of value to future generations, even when they are really not like ballads at all (as in the case of 'At Castle Boterel', with its ababb **rhyme scheme**). Hardy often employs **feminine rhymes**, which might be expected to lighten the poetic mood, but when used in conjunction with **masculine rhymes** (as in 'At Castle Boterel') can generate a wistful and moving effect. He uses **triple rhyme** skilfully in 'The Voice' ('call to me' / 'all to me') to represent the voice of the woman as it comes and goes on the breeze.

Hardy exploits sound patterning – especially **alliteration** – throughout his poetry. A notable example is the triumphant line which concludes 'The Phantom Horsewoman': 'Draws rein and sings to the swing of the tide.' Hardy regularly uses other symmetrical effects, especially **refrains** (as in 'During Wind and Rain') and ballad-like **incremental repetitions** (as in 'The Five Students', where characters drop out as the poem progresses). Throughout Hardy's poetry there is a persistent wish in consciousness – reflected in all aspects of his **versification** – to find pattern (and therefore meaning) in the seemingly random nature of experience, while giving due recognition to the vitality of that randomness. Herein lies the characteristic tension in Hardy's verse, a tension which confers both freshness and, often, thematic ambivalence on individual poems.

Ballad form

In both poems and novels Hardy shows an interest in the vanishing folklore of Wessex (see also Background on Hardy's Wessex), and especially one of its principal forms, the **ballad**. Hardy wrote many ballads and ballad-like poems. The narrative of 'A Trampwoman's Tragedy', for example, is reminiscent of those found in ballads, although the eight-line **stanza** employed is very different from the ballad **quatrain**. The first four lines of each stanza of 'Drummer Hodge' correspond to the ballad quatrain (although Hardy extends it with two extra lines). Often Hardy's use of a limited pattern of **rhyme**, which confers an incantatory effect on the verse, gives a ballad-like feel to poems which are not ballads at all (a striking example of this is 'The Convergence of the Twain'). Elsewhere the use of a **refrain** (in 'A Trampwoman's Tragedy', 'The Five Students' and 'During Wind and Rain', for example) echoes the characteristic manner of ballads.

The ballad form appealed to Hardy for many reasons, not just because it was associated with a Wessex for which he felt deep nostalgia. Ballads were probably a greater influence on his poetry than anything written by his contemporaries: in emulating this style Hardy found another way of resisting the homogeneity of nineteenth-century, middle-class culture. Ballads sprang from the oral tradition – and this satisfied Hardy's preference for the vitality and variety of speech over the fixity of script (and, indeed, over the 'standardised' English which was beginning to erode the **dialects** of rural England). Moreover, in telling their stories, ballads make considerable use of contrasts (life/death, happiness/**tragedy**, past/present, and so on), and this is echoed in the antithetical patterns of Hardy's own poetry – ship/iceberg in 'The Convergence of the Twain', for instance – which were at least in part a challenge to a simplistic, linear, middle-class myth of progress.

The ballad's use of precise but sparing detail and an **impersonal** narrative style accorded with Hardy's own inclination towards reticence – but these characteristics also gave them a universality which he hoped to achieve in his own work. As Hardy realised, however, ballads are paradoxically both timeless *and* rooted in the past. On the one hand, they communicate a shared experience – as Hardy notes in 'In Time of "The Breaking of Nations"', where the 'maid and her wight' are seen to be of more lasting human significance than the 'annals' of the First World War. On the other hand, ballads belong to the past – and this gave them a particular appeal for a poet who so often wrote about the passing of time. In fact, unlike traditional ballads, Hardy usually situated his own ballad-like poems in particular times and places (for example, 'A Trampwoman's Tragedy' names several Wessex inns, while in 'The Five Students' Hardy reflects on events in his own life) precisely to underline his concern with transience, the contrast between then and now.

PART FOUR

EXTENDED COMMENTARIES

THE CONVERGENCE OF THE TWAIN (Lines on the loss of the *Titanic*)

Critical readings of this poem have tended to see it as either about human vanity (evinced in the technological arrogance of the ship, and/or the self-indulgence of the rich passengers it was designed for), or about the workings of the iron 'Necessity' which Hardy believed governed the universe (that is, the 'Immanent Will', discussed in Themes).

I

In a solitude of the sea
Deep from human vanity,
And the Pride of Life that planned her, stilly couches she.

II

Steel chambers, late the pyres
Of her salamandrine fires,
Cold currents thrid, and turn to rhythmic tidal lyres.

III

Over the mirrors meant
To glass the opulent
The sea-worm crawls – grotesque, slimed, dumb, indifferent.

IV

Jewels in joy designed
To ravish the sensuous mind
Lie lightless, all their sparkles bleared and black and blind.

V

Dim moon-eyed fishes near
Gaze at the gilded gear
And query: 'What does this vaingloriousness down here?' ...

5

10

15

VI

Well: while was fashioning
This creature of cleaving wing,
The Immanent Will that stirs and urges everything

VII

Prepared a sinister mate
For her – so gaily great –   20
A Shape of Ice, for the time far and dissociate.

VIII

And as the smart ship grew
In stature, grace, and hue,
In shadowy silent distance grew the Iceberg too.

IX

Alien they seemed to be: 25
No mortal eye could see
The intimate welding of their later history,

X

Or sign that they were bent
By paths coincident
On being anon twin halves of one august event,   30

XI

Till the Spinner of the Years
Said 'Now!' And each one hears,
And consummation comes, and jars two hemispheres.

'Vanity' was a favourite word of Hardy's to describe nineteenth-century selfishness and egotism, and the pursuit of wealth and pleasure. Thus he doesn't use the word in its superficial modern sense (personal self-regard) but with portentous biblical associations (for example, the preacher in Ecclesiastes I describes 'all the works that are done under the sun' as 'vanity'). Certainly the opening **stanzas** of the poem carefully deploy contrasts to point up the **ironic** end for the *Titanic*, far from the 'vanity' and the 'Pride of Life that planned her'. Employing rich, emotive **diction**, Hardy juxtaposes the great ship with the lowly marine life at the bottom of the sea where it now rests. Its boilers 'turn to rhythmic tidal lyres'. Its mirrors, which were 'meant / To glass the opulent' (Hardy almost seems to take a grim delight in this) are now a place where the 'sea-worm crawls – grotesque, slimed, dumb, indifferent'. The 'Jewels' in the ship's extravagant décor lie 'lightless, all their sparkles bleared and black and blind'. No wonder fishes stare at the 'gilded gear' and ask ' "What does this vaingloriousness down here?" ' (ironically, the question that everyone was asking at the time).

The evidence of the opening stanzas does tend to suggest that Hardy was more critical of the ship's ostentation than its engineering (which he actually seems to have been impressed by). But in any case this is really only half the story of the poem, for from stanza VI onwards we get its controlling ironic counterpoint: the ship was being constructed at the same time that the 'Immanent Will' was shaping the iceberg (described in appropriately austere language: 'sinister', 'dissociate', 'shadowy silent') which was to sink it. Hardy emphasises that no human could have predicted this catastrophe, issuing as it did from processes so apparently unrelated.

Is it possible to reconcile the varying critical readings of this poem? Did human beings bring this disaster on themselves because of their 'vanity', or was the sinking of the ship the result of the workings of Necessity, or (to set aside Hardy's abstractions for a moment) pure coincidence? It seems that the poem might be raising the question of whether human beings make their own history or whether it is shaped by external forces. Closer examination of the poem shows that it is deeply ambiguous about these issues.

The poem's ambiguities reside to a considerable extent in the hidden meanings of the words it employs. Again and again Hardy uses words which convey an antithetical sense of things being either self-willed (that is, expressing vanity) or shaped by external forces (that is, directed by the Immanent Will, or fate, part of some pre-ordained plan). Thus the *Titanic* is described as 'smart' (line 22), which means both 'stylish, fashionable' and (an older meaning) 'stinging, painful', referring especially to 'the pain resulting from punishment for some wrongdoing' (in this case, perhaps vanity) by an external agent. Ship and iceberg are described as being 'bent' on collision (line 28): 'bent' can either mean 'determined, self-willed' or 'directed by an external force'. Ship and iceberg are seen as being on 'paths coincident' (line 29): 'coincident' can mean 'occurring together' (brought about by individual actions) or 'in agreement' (indicating an underlying unity or plan). The collision takes place 'anon' (line 30) which can mean 'soon' (that is, at some unspecified time of an individual's choice) or (an even older meaning) 'in unity' or 'in one course or direction' (that is, planned for a certain time). The collision is described as an 'august event' (line 30): 'august' means 'impressive, imposing' but also brings to mind the word 'augury' (that is, an omen which is subsequently brought to fruition).

Ambiguity, then, is the keynote of this poem. It might seem that Hardy is raising (without attempting to resolve) alternative possibilities: either there is an external fate operating in the world which led to the sinking of the *Titanic*, or human vanity was to blame. But there is a third possibility, which is that Hardy thought that humanity was both the prisoner of the web of fate *and* the maker of its own destiny. Or to put it another way, reckless behaviour in a world of chance and time invariably ends in disaster (as is often the case in Hardy's novels).

Hardy certainly thought for a time that collective human effort and determination might influence the Immanent Will and make the world a better place: this hope formed part of his 'evolutionary meliorism' (see Themes). And is it not possible therefore that he thought the obverse was true – that human blindness could provoke fate by stirring the Immanent Will to malign intervention? The First World War shattered Hardy's hopes for humanity and there is in his last poems (such as ' "We Are Getting to the End" ' and 'He Resolves to Say No More') an even bleaker perception of the workings of Necessity as well as a deepening sense of exasperation with the folly of the human race. That the two might be linked is explored in 'The Convergence of the Twain'.

If this is the case it goes some way to explaining a further ambiguity in the poem. There is an extended **metaphor** of marriage working through the last five stanzas. At first this seems odd. In stanza VII the iceberg is described as a 'sinister mate' for the *Titanic*. Stanza IX predicts their 'intimate welding'. In stanza X iceberg and ship are described as 'twin halves of one august event' which achieve 'consummation' (which can mean both 'completion' and 'sexual union in marriage') in stanza XI. If there is a link between the Immanent Will and human actions, then the title of the poem signifies not just the collision of iceberg and ship, but the catastrophic union of vanity and fate.

Finally, the ambiguities of the poem extend to its **metrical** features. The **rhythmic** precision of the poem (striking when read out loud) is meant to emulate the superb engineering of the ship (the vanity which built her), but in its forward drive it also catches that inexorable process which leads to the fated collision with the iceberg (the forces of the universe which destroyed her). Each stanza comprises two **trimeters** and one **hexameter**. For the most part strongly **iambic**, these lines echo the rhythm of the ship's pistons, but the occasional, carefully placed **anapaest** and the release into the long third line also suggest the movement of the ship through the water. Indeed, it has often been pointed out that the shape of each stanza resembles a ship lying low in the water.

AT CASTLE BOTEREL

'After a Journey', 'Beeny Cliff' and 'At Castle Boterel' form the core of the *Poems of 1912–13*, the sequence of **elegies** Hardy wrote following the death of his wife Emma. After the earlier poems expressing shock and grief, they represent that stage in the elegiac **cycle** when the bereaved person seeks recovery by imagining an ideal **image** of the loved one to compensate for the painful fact of death. 'At Castle Boterel' is Hardy's most convincing attempt to reclaim the past by envisioning the youthful Emma in the landscape of their idyllic courtship (he had undertaken a pilgrimage to Cornwall in 'search' of her). Some commentators have suggested that in this poem love does indeed conquer time, but it may in fact be better to read it as a poem of both reclamation and loss.

> As I drive to the junction of lane and highway,
>> And the drizzle bedrenches the waggonette,
> I look behind at the fading byway,
>> And see on its slope, now glistening wet,
>>> Distinctly yet   5

Myself and a girlish form benighted
    In dry March weather. We climb the road
Beside a chaise. We had just alighted
    To ease the sturdy pony's load
        When he sighed and slowed.   10

What we did as we climbed, and what we talked of
    Matters not much, nor to what it led, –
Something that life will not be balked of
    Without rude reason till hope is dead,
        And feeling fled.   15

It filled but a minute. But was there ever
    A time of such quality, since or before,
In that hill's story? To one mind never,
    Though it has been climbed, foot-swift, foot-sore,
        By thousands more.   20

Primaeval rocks form the road's steep border,
    And much have they faced there, first and last,
Of the transitory in Earth's long order;
    But what they record in colour and cast
        Is – that we two passed.   25

And to me, though Time's unflinching rigour,
    In mindless rote, has ruled from sight
The substance now, one phantom figure
    Remains on the slope, as when that night
        Saw us alight.   30

I look and see it there, shrinking, shrinking,
    I look back at it amid the rain
For the very last time; for my sand is sinking,
    And I shall traverse old love's domain
        Never again.   35

March 1913

The opening **stanza** contains a reference to another quester in pursuit of a wife who has died. 'I look behind' says Hardy – as did Orpheus, who, in ancient myth, set out on a quest to recover his wife from the underworld. In Orpheus's case the backward glance as he is about to leave Hades proves disastrous: he loses Eurydice forever. Here it looks as though Hardy's quest is going to fail too: he is about to leave the scenes of his courtship, never to return. But just at the moment of departure he pauses to look back and is rewarded by a vision of himself and Emma on the hillside.

Hardy's initial sense of failure is suggested by the drizzle which 'bedrenches the waggonette'. But in fact the mist becomes an aid to vision by clouding the reality of the scene behind him ('the fading byway') and enabling a shift into memory and the past (which is what his 'look behind' has now become). Thus he envisions 'Distinctly' – and the memory of 'Myself and a girlish form' is given substance by the recollected physicality of their ascent of the hill all those years ago: the pony was 'sturdy' but the lovers had to alight and make the effort of the climb themselves.

This is a sign, after the hesitant opening of the poem, that Hardy's confidence is growing. The challenge he has set himself here is to convince the reader that the subjective memory (the presence of the two lovers on the hillside and what they stood for) can transcend the objective facts of time and space. The process begins in earnest with a paradox: what they did on the hillside is of little consequence – but he says there never was a 'time of such quality ... In that hill's story'. Indeed, though many other walkers have made the ascent ('it has been climbed, foot-swift, foot-sore, / By thousands more') their story is unique.

This paradox forms the basis of what is to follow, and much of the power of the poem rests in Hardy's struggle with the contradictions of mind and matter: the landscape is mindless but endures, while human beings have consciousness (the power to love and remember, for example) but are ephemeral. And Hardy does not flinch from recognising that the forces of the universe are ranged against them. There is a keen sense in this poem (as elsewhere) of the intractability of the material world:

> Primaeval rocks form the road's steep border,
>   And much have they faced there, first and last,
> Of the transitory in Earth's long order

The landscape endures while the human beings ('the transitory in Earth's long order') are here today and gone tomorrow. But consciousness, subjective perception – the capacity of the mind to reclaim the past, and invest the landscape with meaning – can challenge those objective facts.

Hardy clinches his point with an astonishing assertion. With an **ironic allusion** to the fossil record which formed part of the supporting evidence for Charles Darwin's argument, he says the rocks themselves still bear traces of the fact that he and Emma were there: 'what they record in colour and cast / Is – that we two passed.' This is delivered with such conviction, coming where it does in the poem's structure, that we are inclined to believe him. The lovers who were once on that hillside, and Hardy by recalling them, have challenged the passage of time and transformed the enduring landscape.

This enables Hardy to move to the poem's crowning expression of faith. While again acknowledging the objective fact – 'Time's unflinching rigour, / In mindless rote, has ruled from sight / The substance now' – his subjective perception is that Emma's 'phantom figure' still remains on the slope. Of course, by any objective standard this is not true; but the illusion is sustained here (although the use of the word 'phantom' quietly reminds the reader, even at this triumphant moment, that it *is* an illusion). Time and space can be measured (and the poem insists on this again and again, for example, 'but a minute', 'ever', 'first and last', and so on), but there is a human, subjective truth – Hardy calls it 'quality' – which transcends mindless matter.

But can love really be said to conquer time in this poem? If so, the reader feels its victory is only momentary. Indeed, this impression is reinforced by the structure of the poem, which moves from the hesitant opening (present), through the growing confidence of the middle section and the vision of the young, beautiful Emma (past), to the faltering, sad conclusion (present). At the end of the poem Hardy reminds us that he is old (his 'sand is sinking') and he takes a final look back at the 'phantom' which is 'shrinking, shrinking' – away from the rain of present reality and the fading light into the past and the grave; and perhaps too, somewhat reproachfully, away from Hardy's attempts at reconciliation on the basis of reawakened love. The simultaneity of past and present in the poem has the effect of emphasising the real sense of loss which returns at the end. For the truth is that Time has been doubly destructive in this story: first it killed the love between the couple (the estrangement in their marriage) and then it killed Emma. This gives force to Hardy's final remark: 'I shall traverse old love's domain / Never again.'

The recovery from grief which concludes the **elegiac cycle** and which here depends upon the envisioning of Emma is achieved only after a struggle in consciousness. This is the final impression which the poem leaves, despite its confident middle section. Ground is won, then lost. This is echoed in the **rhythms** of the poem, which betray a tension between conviction and doubt, recovery and loss. Each stanza moves from constraint and hesitation (suggested in the mid-line pauses or **caesurae**, and the alternating **masculine** and **feminine endings** in the first four lines of each stanza) to release in the short final line, where conviction and faith prevail. Until, that is, the final short line of the seventh stanza, which seems to shut the door on love and vision with equal certainty.

DURING WIND AND RAIN

Hardy considered 'During Wind and Rain' to be among his best and many critics have endorsed this view. It is an ambivalent poem which has prompted some very different readings. It certainly shows a poignant awareness of the effects of time and change – but how successful is it in resisting those processes?

> They sing their dearest songs –
> He, she, all of them – yea,
> Treble and tenor and bass,
>   And one to play;
> With the candles mooning each face ...   5
>   Ah, no; the years O!
> How the sick leaves reel down in throngs!
>
> They clear the creeping moss –
> Elders and juniors – aye,
> Making the pathways neat   10
>   And the garden gay;
> And they build a shady seat ...
>   Ah, no; the years, the years;
> See, the white storm-birds wing across!

> They are blithely breakfasting all –   15
> Men and maidens – yea,
> Under the summer tree,
>   With a glimpse of the bay,
> While pet fowl come to the knee ...
>   Ah, no; the years O!   20
> And the rotten rose is ript from the wall.
>
> They change to a high new house,
> He, she, all of them – aye,
> Clocks and carpets and chairs
>   On the lawn all day,   25
> And brightest things that are theirs ...
>   Ah, no; the years, the years;
> Down their carved names the rain-drop ploughs.

This poem is retrospective – the past is seen from the perspective of the present. Nevertheless, the whole poem is conducted in the present tense, which suggests the simultaneity in the poet's mind of then and now and reinforces the sense of the passage of time. This tends also to unsettle any simple conclusion that the past is better than the present (which might otherwise seem obvious here). The poem seems to offer a backward glance over a whole life from the vantage point of old age, with the impulse to trace out meaningful patterns. But even by Hardy's standards the narrative restraint in this poem is striking: we are never told who 'they' are. This may be a self-protective manoeuvre, but it certainly has the effect of universalising the experience.

The poem offers a series of **images** of ordinary human beings engaged in the everyday activities of family life – singing, tidying the garden and building a 'shady seat', having breakfast on the lawn, moving house. But all this is set in the context of the 'years' and at the end of the poem we realise that 'they' are all dead. There seem to be two versions of time active in the poem: ordinary, everyday time within which the business of family life is conducted, and 'Time' – inhuman, cosmic, a fundamental principle of the material universe – which provides the more alien framework within which these activities and lives take place. This is the source of much of the poem's ambivalence.

Each stanza has the same antithetical pattern, setting the positive, social, daily activities of the human family against the destructive processes of Time. In part the contrasts are located in the verbs employed as well as the concepts. The family 'sing' (an image of harmony and fellowship); they 'clear' and 'build' (an image of shared work); they are seen 'breakfasting' on the lawn (as if such days will last forever); they 'change' house (a normal part of a family history). But the **ballad**-like **refrain** on the sixth line of each stanza abruptly reminds us of the passing years, and introduces the changes they have wrought: the 'sick leaves reel down in throngs', the 'white storm-birds wing across', the 'rotten rose is ript from the wall', and finally 'the rain-drop ploughs' down the names carved on the tombstones. In each case the single destructive verb of the last line is juxtaposed with the earlier creative verbs. The impact of the last line, and of the refrain which precedes it, is enhanced by a change in the **rhythm**. After the easy-going movement of the first five lines (which confers an informed, lively tone), the refrain is slow and sombre, and it sets up the long final line with its four heavy **stresses**. The **alliteration** and **assonance** which reinforce the (creative) rhythmic qualities of the opening lines of each stanza ('They sing their dearest songs', 'They clear the creeping moss') have a quite different effect in the final lines, where they emphasise the destructiveness of Time ('See, the white storm-birds wing across!', 'And the rotten rose is ript from the wall'). And the contrast between past and present, between order and chaos, between the familiar and the alien, is highlighted by the return to the opening **rhyme** at the end of each stanza.

However, the first five lines of each stanza are not entirely immune from the changes which the last two lines confirm: all the activities described take place in a domestic time, but a careful reading might well reveal a sense of fundamental 'Time' in some of the details mentioned. Thus an evening of family singing is recalled: 'Treble and tenor and bass, / And one to play'. But the reference to 'candles mooning each face' brings to mind the traditional **image** of a burning candle representing the transience of life. We hear about work in the garden (clearing the paths and building a seat), but the reference to the 'creeping moss' reminds us of the way nature can reclaim the sites of human endeavour. They breakfast on the lawn in summer, but the word 'blithely' perhaps suggests a complacency about the effects of Time. 'They change to a high new house' – but it is significant that Hardy chooses the verb 'change' and not 'move'. Finally, the description of the furniture on the lawn prompts thought of other occasions when this might be so – following a death, for instance.

Perhaps Hardy is simply saying that, in a characteristically human way, the family carry on with their lives, for the most part regardless of the fact that they live in a universe of Time and change. The last lines of each stanza undermine this complacency, but the contradictions are managed without **irony** here – or at least the irony is muted. The truth is that they all have died; but their lives, their energy and hopes, their purpose and fellowship ('brightest things that are theirs') which are solidly present in each stanza are not negated by this fact. And this is as true for humans now as it ever was. Hardy's journey into memory, his reclaiming of the past, is a way of rewinning the present, reminding us of what matters, and resisting the **alienating** effects of Time.

Not every reader would agree with this interpretation. Some critics point to the title and say that the wind and rain stand as the controlling **symbols** in a poem of change and decay, suffering and loss. This symbolism is emphasised in the last line of each stanza. The wind makes the 'sick leaves reel down in throngs' – the falling leaves of autumn are a traditional **image** for Time and mortality. The 'white storm-birds' are harbingers of death hovering over the tidied garden. The 'rotten rose is ript', by the malevolence of Time, from the wall near where the family were 'blithely breakfasting'. And all this leads to the final image of the gravestones. Moreover, some critics say the poem also asserts that the past was better than the present, for that is where all the music was to be found.

One way of resolving these different readings is to look carefully at the last stanza. On the face of it the live songs of the opening stanza have been reduced to the dead inscriptions on the tombstones, and there is no doubt that this is one of the meanings of the poem. The preceding stanzas might have conveyed a sense that the individuals mentioned would go on forever, but the truth is that even those busy lives were short and ended in the grave: 'Down their carved names the rain-drop ploughs.' The use of the word 'plough' is surprising here. At first it seems that nature (Time) is slowly erasing the record of those names, having already erased the lives themselves. But 'plough' is also an **image** of human labour and of regeneration (compare a similar idea in the poem 'In Time of "The Breaking of Nations" '). And here it is linked with language, the 'carved names'. In this way the tombstones become an ambivalent image, not only of death, but of the antidote to Time and change – the resilience of the human community, of work, language, and the importance of memory. Thus an image of destruction is transformed into an image of renewal and in so doing validates the theme and form of the poem itself.

PART FIVE

BACKGROUND

THOMAS HARDY'S LIFE

Thomas Hardy is perhaps best known as a major **Victorian** novelist. He had written poetry as a young man but achieved literary prominence as the writer of novels such as *Far from the Madding Crowd* (1874), *The Mayor of Casterbridge* (1886) and *Tess of the d'Urbervilles* (1891). In 1895, following the publication of *Jude the Obscure*, he abandoned novel-writing altogether and returned to what he claimed was his first love – the writing of poetry. Between the age of fifty-five and his death at eighty-seven in 1928, Hardy published over 900 poems and these, by his own account, comprised only a fraction of what he wrote.

Hardy was born in 1840 in the Dorset hamlet of Higher Bockhampton, near Dorchester (see also Chronology). His father was a builder and master mason, and from him Thomas inherited a love of music; his mother, who had worked as a servant before marrying, encouraged her son's literary tastes. Hardy attended school in Dorchester before being apprenticed at sixteen to a local architect. During this period he met and became friendly with the **dialect**-poet and parson William Barnes (commemorated in 'The Last Signal'), and also Horace Moule, who became his literary mentor but who committed suicide in 1873 (see 'The Five Students' and 'Standing by the Mantelpiece'). Hardy, an excessively shy but ambitious young man, moved to London in 1862 to work for a firm of architects and stayed there for five years. During this period he read intensively and wrote poems. He considered going to theological college to train for the Church, but in fact his faith dissolved when subjected to the necessary scrutiny this entailed. The strain of this experience seems to have affected his health and in 1867 he returned to Dorchester, where he again found work as an architect.

At this time he began to write his first (unpublished) novel and fell in love with the sixteen-year-old Tryphena Sparks, who was regarded as his cousin but may have been his niece. There has been much (inconclusive) speculation about this relationship, but whatever its exact nature it seems clear that its failure deeply affected Hardy. In 1868 he went to St Juliot in

Cornwall, to undertake the restoration of a church, and met the rector's sister-in-law, Emma Gifford. His first published novel, *Desperate Remedies*, appeared in 1871, to be followed by *Under the Greenwood Tree* (1872) and *Far from the Madding Crowd* (1874). This was his first great success, and on the strength of it he decided to give up architecture, become a full-time writer and marry Emma. Twelve other novels followed and many short stories. By 1880 Hardy was a celebrity frequenting London's literary and aristocratic circles, although often rather ill at ease while doing so. In 1885 the Hardys moved into Max Gate, near Dorchester, a house Hardy had designed himself. Ten years later Hardy wrote his last novel and began to prepare his first volume of poetry.

Why did Hardy abandon novel-writing? He claimed that it was largely because of the hostile reception received by both *Tess of the d'Urbervilles* and *Jude the Obscure*. Both novels were condemned as immoral: *Tess of the d'Urbervilles* shocked respectable opinion with its depiction of rape, illegitimate birth and adultery, while *Jude the Obscure* caused further outrage with its treatment of the 'deadly war waged between flesh and spirit' (in the preface to the 1912 edition, Hardy recounts how the work was 'burnt by a bishop – probably in his despair at not being able to burn me'). A related factor was the opposition of his wife, Emma, to the publication of the latter novel (she actually tried to block it). Things had not been good between the Hardys for some time but Emma felt doubly betrayed by *Jude the Obscure*: it offended her evangelical religious sensibilities and, in attacking the institution of marriage, seemed to offer her own union with her husband up to public scrutiny. It is possible, too, that Hardy felt as uncomfortable about approval of these later outspoken novels as he did about condemnation. Temperamentally shy and retiring – for all his burning literary ambition – and, paradoxically, morbidly sensitive to Victorian proprieties, Hardy recoiled from being seen as a leader of free thinking.

Public and private difficulties, therefore, conspired to plunge Hardy into personal crisis and depression in 1895–6, by which time he had become a virtual recluse at his home in Dorchester. The 'In Tenebris' poems, and others from this time, reflect his state of mind. Initially, he probably resorted to writing poems as a kind of self-therapy – as well as the fact that he simply enjoyed writing them. But the truth is that Hardy soon came to take his career as a poet very seriously indeed: he subsequently promoted the view that this was the most important phase of his literary career.

Hardy spent hours in the reading room of the British Museum studying the works of his poetic predecessors, one of the fruits of this research being the huge range of **metrical** styles and **verse forms** employed in his poems. He awaited the reviews in a state of high nervous tension and was bitterly disappointed if they were critical, as many of the early ones were. But as volume followed volume (there were eight between 1898 and 1928) his confidence grew and the reviews got better. In addition, the three parts of *The Dynasts, an epic-drama of the War with Napoleon* appeared in 1903, 1906 and 1908. This made a major contribution to his rising status as a poet, something confirmed when the King awarded him the Order of Merit in 1910.

Emma died in 1912. The strains in the Hardys' marriage had been evident since the 1870s as Emma's natural vitality jarred increasingly with her husband's reticence. But Hardy was deeply shocked by her death and out of his grief and guilt emerged the famous *Poems of 1912–13*. In 1914 Hardy, now aged seventy-four, married Florence Dugdale, who had for some time been his housekeeper and secretary. She was nearly forty years his junior. Public recognition continued to come his way, including honorary degrees from Oxford and Cambridge, a visit from the Prince of Wales, and the Gold Medal of the Royal Society of Literature.

Thomas Hardy died in January 1928. His ashes were buried in Westminster Abbey and his heart in his first wife's grave in Stinsford churchyard, near Higher Bockhampton. In 1917 he had begun his autobiography. This was eventually published posthumously, under his second wife's name, as *The Early Life of Thomas Hardy, 1840–1891* (1928) and *The Later Years of Thomas Hardy, 1892–1928* (1930). This was a curious but revealing attempt to pass on to posterity the 'authorised' (and respectable) version of his life, for it suppressed some uncomfortable personal details (including the relationship with Tryphena Sparks). Indeed, in the years prior to his death Hardy had, with Florence's help, made a determined effort to draw a veil over much of his life by destroying many letters and personal writings.

At the time of Hardy's birth, traditional and customary ways of life were still practised in Dorset, which was as yet almost completely untouched by the incursions of industrialism, or the railway (which did not reach the valley of the Frome until Hardy was eight years old). By the time of his death in 1928 the world had changed completely: there were cars, aeroplanes (in ' "And There Was a Great Calm" ' he calls them 'weft-winged engines'), movies, telephones, radios and television.

However, although Hardy lived on into the twentieth century, his intellectually formative years – the ones which were to determine the characteristic mood of his poetry – were those of his youth and young manhood in the late 1850s, the 1860s and the early 1870s. The earlier part of this period marked the high point of **Victorian** middle-class industrial and commercial civilisation. After the Great Exhibition of 1851, middle-class Britons enjoyed a period of unprecedented material prosperity based on unmatched industrial and agricultural production, and social and political stability. Their buoyant, sometimes arrogant, mood lasted for twenty years, although long before 1870 the factors which were to unsettle that confidence were already taking shape.

Hardy was very critical of this expanding, materialistic middle-class culture, but he was also a man of his time. While he disliked the ethics of capitalism – saying the rich man was usually 'as coldblooded as a fish and as selfish as a pig' – he was nevertheless ambitious himself and hoped for fame and fortune. He hated privilege and the injustices of a class society but married a woman from a class higher than his own and, after his novels made him famous, mixed on equal terms with politicians and members of the nobility. He was dismayed by the irresistible onward march of 'Progress' which was **symbolised** for him by the railway pushing into Dorset and changing forever ancient patterns of country life. But he remained fascinated all his life by developments in industry, science and technology.

Hardy was particularly dismayed by the impact of capitalism on rural communities. Mechanisation was cost-effective and produced bigger crops, but it also increased rural unemployment, and destroyed village traditions and continuity as dispossessed labourers were forced to wander the countryside looking for work. He was acutely aware of what was being lost under the pressures of homogenisation and centralisation. He had ambivalent feelings about the Education Act of 1870 and the introduction of a national system of schooling: this might increase opportunities for rural children but it also accelerated the eradication of the Dorset **dialect**. Resistance to these processes – and, by implication, to middle-class society as a whole – can be found in both the use of dialect and the adaptation of the **ballad** form (see Techniques) in Hardy's poetry, as well as the recreation of pre-industrial ways of life in both his poetry and his novels.

After 1870, however, Victorian middle-class civilisation itself seemed to lose its way. The change of mood was largely due to a loss of economic confidence because of industrial competition from Germany and the USA. Moreover, there were growing anxieties about political instability and social unrest: there was widespread fear of the 'masses' fuelled by violence in urban centres (for example, the Hyde Park Riots in 1866, the Siege of Paris in 1870 and the Paris Commune of 1871). These developments prompted a more general **ideological** crisis which had in fact been simmering away for some years. The fragmentation of Victorian culture after 1870 followed from the crumbling of many of the cherished beliefs – about religion, history, politics, gender, and so on – which had underpinned the successes of middle-class society.

Hardy, as might be expected, was very receptive to challenges to the received wisdom of the age, but again, it must be remembered, he was a man of his time and his enthusiasm for the new ideas was, as with many of his contemporaries, not always completely consistent. Thus, like many people after the publication of Darwin's *Origin of Species* (1859), Hardy lost his faith and became a vigorous critic of organised religion and its institutions (particularly marriage), but he retained a religious sense all his life and continued to look to the Bible as a source of ethical wisdom. After Darwin, many Victorians felt themselves to be the victims of time, as it was now difficult to believe that history had a design and purpose (i.e. that there was a divine Providence at work in the world ensuring the triumph of the Victorian middle classes), but while this confirmed what Hardy already felt, he continued to search for patterns in both history and his own personal life (see Themes). In politics, socialism emerged as an active force in British political life after 1880 but although Hardy clearly was sympathetic, he moved in elite circles during his London years and joined no political movement. The nature of women's role in society was widely debated in the last quarter of the nineteenth century, reaching a peak in the 1890s (the debate was fuelled by the 'death of God' and the undermining of patriarchal notions, and legislation which improved women's rights). But Hardy's attitude to 'The Woman Question' (as it was called at the time) was ambivalent: while in both his poetry and his novels he does offer sympathetic representations of women, he seems to have retained a very Victorian male tendency to idealise them (as, it might be argued, he does in the *Poems of 1912–13*).

Hardy's quarrel with the middle-class world, then, was genuine if not always consistent. He could be a radical critic of it but part of him longed to succeed in that world and gain its approval. His social, political and religious ideas led to charges that he was angry, immoral and subversive. But the enthusiasm of other radicals for his ideas made him feel uneasy: one of the reasons he gave up writing novels was that he didn't want to be considered a leader of free thinkers. Hardy valued respectability and this motive informs the authorised version of his life in the 'biography' which purports to be by his second wife, Florence, but which in fact he wrote himself.

The last vestiges of Victorianism were swept away by major wars: the (second) Boer War (1899–1902), when Dutch farmers fought Britain for control of South Africa, and the First World War (1914–18). Hardy found the 'jingoism' (aggressive nationalism and xenophobia) which was associated with both conflicts repugnant and as a consequence was attacked for writing un-British, unpatriotic poems (see 'In Tenebris II' and 'The Pity of It'). He was not a pacifist, however, and supported the war against Germany, hoping that this would indeed be 'the war to end wars'. But his final years saw the rise of the European dictators and in his last poems he gloomily predicted further hostilities.

HARDY'S WESSEX

'Wessex Heights' is often seen as the poem which marks Hardy's renunciation of novel-writing and commitment to poetry following the uproar which greeted *Jude the Obscure* (see Thomas Hardy's Life). The four hills named in this poem mark out, approximately, the ancient kingdom of Wessex which Hardy uses as the setting of most of his novels and many of his poems. Hardy's fictionalised Wessex is centred on Dorset, and particularly Dorchester (which he called 'Casterbridge'). Wessex first appears in *Far from the Madding Crowd*, and its topography is fully delineated in subsequent novels. In 'Wessex Heights' Hardy announces that the region will also be his poetic domain.

Historically, Wessex was one of the seven kingdoms of the Anglo-Saxons (specifically, the territory of the West Saxons) following Britain's separation from the Roman Empire around AD500. It probably covered the present-day counties of Hampshire, Dorset, Wiltshire, Berkshire, Somerset and Devon, and its main centres were Winchester and Southampton. Wessex reached the height of its power in the tenth century (by now including Kent and Sussex) after the rule of its best-known king, Alfred the Great. Alfred was alone amongst the Anglo-Saxon kings in successfully resisting the raids of the Vikings; his successors fought to regain the land the Vikings had conquered (the 'Danelaw') and eventually united all England (literally 'land of the Angles') under a single monarchy in AD954.

For Hardy, though, Wessex was as much a landscape of the mind as it was a place with a social and historical reality. He himself said that Wessex was 'partly real, partly dream'. In many ways a **symbolic** landscape, it represented Hardy's sense of the inexorable passage of time (in both its long, many-layered history as well as Hardy's personal experiences) and the indifference of nature (a place where generations of transient human beings, including his own family, had lived and died). It was a site, then, where past and present rubbed against each other, where human vulnerability was continually reiterated (the sources of **alienation**) – but where community life and individual memory (the patterning impulses of consciousness) offered resistance to the bleak and meaningless realities of space and time. In this respect, Hardy's imagined Wessex externalised his mental landscape.

This is not to say, however, that Hardy was not acutely aware of the real problems of contemporary Wessex. He felt a genuine fellowship with agricultural workers – this is reflected in 'Drummer Hodge', where the **elegiac** form of the poem itself challenges those class attitudes which had led to a scandalous neglect of rural hardship. But above all, perhaps, Hardy saw himself as a historian of a valued, and ancient, way of life in a region which was being disrupted by nineteenth-century social and economic change (see Historical Background). Thus in the poems we find a wish to record for posterity details, both personal and public, of that threatened culture: family traditions ('The Self-Unseeing'), folk-tales ('The Oxen'), the

Dorsetshire **dialect** ('The Pity of It'), local events (the Dorchester fair in 'Exeunt Omnes') as well as, more generally, the recurring patterns of rural life and work ('In Time of "The Breaking of Nations" ', 'During Wind and Rain').

Hardy understood the dangers of this kind of commemoration of a disappearing Wessex – specifically, the temptation to romanticise the region for a sophisticated, and largely urban, readership (on whom, after all, he depended for his livelihood). Indeed, this kind of criticism has been levelled at the portrayal of Wessex in his novels. However, Hardy actively resists this charge in his poems, where, as has been suggested, he felt able to express his real opinions more freely: in a poem such as 'The Darkling Thrush', for example, he is quite uncompromising in his depiction of the harsher aspects of Wessex and a landscape which is merely 'haunted' by humankind.

LITERARY BACKGROUND

W.H. Auden said of Hardy that 'he was modern without being too modern', an ambivalence which highlights the difficulty in placing Hardy in literary history. Born in 1840, Hardy might seem to be in origin a **Victorian** (although the accident of birth isn't necessarily a sound basis for determining literary style). But latterly he was a contemporary of the **modernist** poets – T.S. Eliot, Ezra Pound and W.B. Yeats – who were at the height of their powers while he was still alive.

So, in literary terms, to what extent is it appropriate to speak of Hardy as a Victorian? What evidence is there of modernism in his work? Is it better to think of him as a transitional figure between these two literary periods? Or should we attempt to formulate a quite different way of placing Hardy – one which is somewhat outside the mainstream literary movements and accepted critical categories?

There is little evidence that Hardy's poetic practice or theory was significantly influenced by other **Victorian** poets. However, his extensive reading and research resulted in poems which contain numerous references and **allusions** to other poets, both of the nineteenth century and earlier. Critics have pointed out particular debts to Robert Browning, whose tough-minded philosophical poetry, interest in history and exploitation of the **dramatic monologue** appealed to Hardy. Similarly, Tennyson's **elegiac** style and melancholy reflections on the passage of time may have played some part in shaping Hardy's characteristic manner.

But often one feels that it is other writers' *ideas* rather than their practice which have the most influence on Hardy's work – which, in terms of style, remains idiosyncratically his own. For example, Hardy admired Swinburne's 'musical' poetry – but seems to have been even more impressed by his unconventional ideas on religion, politics and sex (notably, a very un-Victorian interest in passion). Hardy shared Swinburne's pessimism: both writers thought that the universe was indifferent to human hopes and aspiration and that the only hope for betterment lay in the collective efforts of humankind. Hardy also felt that Swinburne had been treated harshly by public opinion, just like himself (see Thomas Hardy's Life on the reception of his last two novels).

On the other hand, some critics have endeavoured to find traces of **modernism** in Hardy's poetry, saying that it evinces anti-Victorian tendencies everywhere, in style as well as theme. Ezra Pound found specifically **imagist** qualities in Hardy's work, and critics point to 'Snow in the Suburbs' as the best example of this. Others have found a more general modernist flavour in Hardy's deliberate disruption of **metrical** patterns, his **syntactic** eccentricities, his **neologisms**, his mixing of **colloquial** and literary **diction**, his sudden shifts in tone and so on – in other words, all those stylistic features which constitute Hardy's idiosyncrasy (see Techniques). Hardy distrusted written language for the same reason as the modernists, fearing that it might slide into lifeless fixity – he sought to give his poems an asymmetry which would preserve their freshness.

It has also been suggested that Hardy echoes the anti-**Romantic** stance of the modernists. Eliot, Pound and Yeats all endeavoured to write **impersonally**, from perspectives not necessarily their own. They rejected the Wordsworthian '**egotistical sublime**' where a poet's preoccupation with his or her own life, thoughts and feelings is the very essence of the poet's work. One might object that this is precisely why T.S. Eliot had so little time for Hardy, a writer who seems to have accepted that the proper subject of his poetry was his own life. But as shown in the Commentaries, although Hardy writes out of his own experience, he does so with a surprising degree of reticence that prevents the reader getting close to him. This seems to have much in common with Yeats's adoption of masks, in poems akin to **dramatic monologues** where the speaker is clearly not the poet, or Eliot's assumption of different **personae** in *The Waste Land* (1922). Thus Hardy shares the modernist suspicion of Romantic soul-bearing.

The problem with this is that although Hardy may be to some extent arguing with his Romantic inheritance – in ways which give his poetry a modernist flavour – there are other ways in which his debt to the Romantics, and in particular Wordsworth, is clear. Hardy shared Wordsworth's view expressed in 'The Preface' to the 1800 edition of *Lyrical Ballads* that the language proper to poetry is the 'real language of men' – and both writers shared an enthusiasm for **ballads**. Both wrote their poetry out of personal memory (though Wordsworth wrote about his childhood while Hardy recalled his young manhood and days of courtship). Both showed in their poems an affinity for the natural world (though Wordsworth's pantheistic universe is replaced in Hardy by an indifferent one). Both writers valued the representation of endurance in humans as a response to the vicissitudes of experience.

When T.S. Eliot, and some twentieth-century critics, label Hardy a 'Victorian' they do so because of the Romantic qualities of his writing. But they fail to see that his debt bypasses Victorian corruptions of Romanticism (which was their real target) and goes back to the source in Wordsworth himself. In the light of this, it is much more illuminating to think of Hardy's poetry as belonging to a distinctively native English poetic tradition which is neither Victorian nor modernist, which includes Wordsworth, but also poets like John Clare, and has its origins in folk poetry and folk-songs. This indigenous tradition was effectively suppressed during the Victorian period, and prior to Hardy surfaces mainly in the works of William Barnes, the Dorset **dialect**-poet (who knew Hardy personally), and sometimes in Tennyson.

Identifying the features of this native English tradition provides a useful guide to the essential characteristics of Hardy's poetry. It deals with ordinary, everyday experience (the 'maid and her wight' rather than 'War's annals', as 'In Time of "The Breaking of Nations" ' puts it). It is restrained in its treatment and uses the 'real language of men'. It assumes a universality of thoughts and feelings – a contentious notion by the end of the twentieth century, but surely exemplified in poems like 'The Self-Unseeing'. And in any discussion of Hardy's place in a native tradition it is important to recall that his poetry is rooted in the **ballad** form (see Techniques).

While seeing Hardy as a key figure in a native English poetic tradition (see Critical History for further discussion), it is still perfectly valid to regard Hardy the poet as a transitional figure between Victorian and modernist literature. The awareness of human beings as the victims of time and history, which grew in the nineteenth century and is a major theme in Hardy's poetry, is perhaps an even more intense preoccupation of a writer like T.S. Eliot.

PART SIX

CRITICAL HISTORY & FURTHER READING

CRITICAL HISTORY

Thomas Hardy's poetry has never achieved a critical consensus. From the start there were those who recognised the distinctive achievements of his poetry, as well as those (sometimes expressing the prejudice of a metropolitan establishment towards a rural outsider) who found his poems to be both pessimistic and clumsy. But even his admirers have found it difficult to agree on what might constitute the substantial core of his best work: the closest we get to this is perhaps the thirty or forty poems (out of over 900 he published) which editors recurrently choose to include in selections of his poetry (see Note on the Text). Significantly, up until the 1960s it was often practising poets who were most enthusiastic, and most perceptive, about Hardy's poetry. Conversely, during the same period he was neglected or treated with disdain by literary critics who felt that the work of the **modernists** (Ezra Pound, T.S. Eliot and W.B. Yeats) was more important than that of this **Victorian** (as they saw him) who had drifted into the twentieth century.

Hardy has had many admirers among English poets, some of whom have acknowledged a particular debt to him. These include Edward Thomas, Robert Graves, Edmund Blunden, W.H. Auden, Philip Larkin and Cecil Day-Lewis (who, on his death in 1972, was buried, as he had requested, near Hardy's grave in Stinsford churchyard, in recognition of his debt to the poet he acknowledged as having the greatest influence on his own verse). In part this can be seen as evidence of the continuing energy of that native English poetic tradition of which Hardy is an outstanding representative (see Literary Background).

Surprisingly, the American **modernist** poet Ezra Pound claimed that Hardy was a significant influence on his own work: 'Nobody has taught me anything about writing since Thomas Hardy died' (letter, 30 December 1934). But Pound's admiration for Hardy clearly recognises the ways in which he differs from the modernists: poetry, Pound says, can go down one of two roads, that of 'Music' (its **lyric** forms), or 'The old man's road (vide Tom Hardy) – CONTENT, the INSIDES, the subject matter' (letter, 30

October 1934). Thus Pound praises Hardy's poems for their themes (and not treatment, which even he thinks is clumsy) and, interestingly, the retrospective mode in which these themes are delivered ('The old man's road'). Pound could also see that the poetry was, in a sense, the fruit of the earlier fiction: 'Now *there* is clarity. There is the harvest of having written twenty novels first' (letter, April 1937).

W.H. Auden – another poet whose work might at first seem very different from Hardy's – also expresses his indebtedness, but for reasons very different from Pound's. In the essay 'A Literary Transference', which appeared in *Southern Review* 6, summer 1940, Auden says that 'Hardy's faults as a craftsman, his rhythmical clumsiness, his outlandish vocabulary' are obvious but as a consequence he was not an intimidating model to copy. Further, 'no English poet … employed so many complicated stanza forms'. So while Pound says that he was influenced by Hardy's themes and mode, Auden claims that he learnt about form, the mechanics of poetry, from Hardy. But it is an obtuse tribute: Auden somehow fails to see that it is Hardy's idiosyncrasies – even sometimes eccentricities – which confer the power and distinctiveness of his poetic voice.

It was in the 1950s with the work of the so-called **Movement** poets – and in particular the poetry of Philip Larkin – that Hardy gained recognition as the unique representative of a distinctively English tradition who can be invoked as a counterweight to the excesses of **modernism**. Other Movement poets included Kingsley Amis, Donald Davie, Thom Gunn and John Wain. Never a group in any meaningful sense, these poets found common ground in the honesty and lack of sentimentality, the tone of **ironic** detachment, and the avoidance of any romantic posturing, which are so characteristic of Hardy's poetry. They also shared his commitment to the craft of poetry. Donald Davie was in fact to become one of Hardy's most astute critics.

In an essay entitled 'Wanted: Good Hardy Critic' (*Critical Quarterly*, vol. 8, no. 2, summer 1966), Philip Larkin, a poet who was unquestionably influenced by Hardy, lamented the lack of good criticism of his poetic mentor even as he asserted his stature: 'Eliot was hostile, Leavis patronising, Wilson, Empson, Blackmur, Trilling – none has been other than neglectful.' He roundly asserts that 'one reader at least would not wish Hardy's *Collected Poems* a single page shorter, and regards it as many times over the best body of poetry work this century so far has to show'.

The critics Larkin mentions are primarily interested in the poetry of the **modernists**. They tend to see Hardy as a **Victorian** and give him relatively little attention. While there have been attempts to counter this by claiming Hardy for modernism – and some of the arguments are convincing (see Literary Background) – the overall tenor of his work finally resists, as Ezra Pound himself understood, such an appropriation.

F.R. Leavis discusses Hardy in *New Bearings in English Poetry* (Chatto & Windus, 1932, pp. 55–9) and he is at once very shrewd and very narrow in his judgements. His comments can be illuminating. For example, he acknowledges 'that purity of recognition which is Hardy's strength'. He continues by observing that Hardy's poetry 'does what it says, and presents barely the fact recognised by a mind more than commonly responsible and awake'. Elsewhere, however, through a combination of prejudice (against an out-of-date 'Victorian') and contempt (for poetical clumsiness), he proclaims that Hardy was 'a naïve poet of simple attitudes and outlook'. Such conclusions derived in large measure from a conviction that the important twentieth-century poets were Eliot, Pound and Yeats, and for many years Leavis's judgements were very influential. Most damagingly, he perpetrated the myth that Hardy only wrote a 'dozen' good poems, those being 'lost among a vast bulk of verse interesting only by its oddity and idiosyncrasy'. It was precisely this opinion that, thirty years later, Larkin was eager to refute when he said that he would not wish to lose a single poem.

The popularity of Larkin's poetry in the 1960s and 1970s had the related effect of prompting a critical reconsideration of Hardy's poetry. The best of the more recent criticism by Davie, Paulin and Lucas, for example (see Further Reading), is securely founded in a recognition of his place within a native English poetic tradition.

J.O. Bailey, *The Poetry of Thomas Hardy*, University Press of North Carolina, 1970

Poem-by-poem commentaries

R.G. Cox, ed., *Thomas Hardy: The Critical Heritage*, Routledge & Kegan Paul, 1970

Includes early reviews of Hardy's poetry

Donald Davie, *Thomas Hardy and British Poetry*, Oxford University Press, 1972

Illuminating discussion of Hardy's poetry by a poet and academic

Ralph Elliott, *Thomas Hardy's English*, Blackwell, 1984

The most comprehensive guide to Hardy's language

Samuel Hynes, *The Pattern of Hardy's Poetry*, University Press of North Carolina, 1961

Valuable criticism by an eminent Hardy scholar

Trevor Johnson, *A Critical Introduction to the Poems of Thomas Hardy*, Macmillan, 1991

Astute and accessible discussion of Hardy's poetry

Philip Larkin, *Required Writing: Miscellaneous Pieces 1955–1982*, Faber, 1983

Includes the essay 'Wanted: Good Hardy Critic' which originally appeared in *Critical Quarterly*, vol. 8, no. 2, summer 1966

F.R. Leavis, *New Bearings in English Poetry*, Chatto & Windus, 1932

Alternately perceptive and limited discussion of Hardy's poetry which adversely influenced a generation of critical estimations

John Lucas, *Modern English Poetry from Hardy to Hughes*, Batsford, 1986

Includes a good general, if sometimes opinionated, introduction to Hardy

Michael Millgate, *Thomas Hardy: A Biography*, Oxford University Press, 1982

The fullest and most balanced modern biography of Hardy

Michael Millgate, ed., *The Life and Work of Thomas Hardy by F.E. Hardy*, Macmillan, 1985

Claims to be the original text of Hardy's autobiography (*The Early Life* and *The Later Years*) before Florence Hardy altered it for publication

Tom Paulin, *Thomas Hardy: The Poetry of Perception*, Macmillan, 1975
    Excellent account of Hardy's poetic career and craftsmanship

F.B. Pinion, *A Commentary on the Poems of Thomas Hardy*, Macmillan, 1976
    Poem-by-poem commentary including useful background information

Dennis Taylor, *Hardy's Metres and Victorian Prosody*, Macmillan, 1988
    The authoritative work on Hardy's metrics

Dennis Taylor, *Hardy's Poetry 1860–1928*, Clarendon Press, Oxford, 1981
    Astute and illuminating account of Hardy's career and poetic craftsmanship

J.P. Ward, *Thomas Hardy's Poetry*, Open University Press, 1992
    Useful critical introduction to Hardy's poetry

World events	Hardy's life	Poetry
1831-6 Charles Darwin works as unpaid naturalist aboard *The Beagle*		
	1832 Birth of Horace Moule	
1837 Queen Victoria succeeds William IV		
1840 Marriage of Queen Victoria and Prince Albert	**1840** Birth of Hardy at Higher Bockhampton, Dorset, on 2 June; birth of Emma Lavinia Gifford	**1840** Robert Browning, *Sordello*
		1841 Robert Browning, *Pippa Passes*
		1842 Alfred, Lord Tennyson, *Poems*
		1844 William Barnes, *Poems of Rural Life in the Dorset Dialect*
1847 Railway reaches Dorchester		
1848 Revolutionary uprisings throughout mainland Europe	**1848-9** Attends village school in Lower Bockhampton	
	1850-3 Educated at Isaac Last's British School (Nonconformist) in Dorchester	**1850** Death of William Wordsworth; Tennyson, *In Memoriam*
1851 The Great Exhibition is held at the Crystal Palace in London		
	1853-6 Attends Isaac Last's new Congregationalist 'Academy'; starts learning Latin	
1854-6 Crimean War		**1854** Tennyson, 'The Charge of the Light Brigade'
	1856 Apprenticed to ecclesiastical Dorchester architect John Hicks; meets dialect-poet William Barnes	
	1857 Meets Horace Moule; begins to write poetry	
1859 Darwin publishes *On the Origin of Species*		**1859** Edward Fitzgerald, *The Rubáiyát of Omar Khayyám*
	1862 Moves to London to work as an assistant architect for Arthur Blomfield	
		1864 Robert Browning, *Dramatis Personae*

World events	Hardy's life	Poetry
	1865 Abandons plan to train for the Church due to religious doubts	**1865** Algernon Charles Swinburne, *Atalanta in Calydon;* birth of William Butler Yeats
	1867 Returns to Dorchester to work for Hicks again; forms relationship with Tryphena Sparks	**1866** Swinburne, *Poems and Ballads* **1867** Matthew Arnold, *New Poems*
	1869 Works as architect for G.R. Crickmay in Weymouth; possibly engaged to Tryphena Sparks	**1869** Arnold, *Collected Poems;* Tennyson, *The Holy Grail and Other Poems*
1870 Forster's Elementary Education Act sets up school boards	**1870** Meets Emma Gifford while on architectural business in St Juliot, Cornwall; moves to London again to pursue career as architect	
1871 Darwin publishes *The Descent of Man*	**1871** Publication of *Desperate Remedies;* returns to Weymouth to work as architect; trips to Cornwall	**1871** Swinburne, *Songs before Sunrise*
	1872 Works as architect in London; publishes *Under the Greenwood Tree*	
	1873 Publication of *A Pair of Blue Eyes;* becomes engaged to Emma; Moule commits suicide in Cambridge	
	1874 Marriage to Emma; decides to become full-time writer following success of *Far from the Madding Crowd*	
		1875 Swinburne, *Songs of Two Nations;* Tennyson, *The Lover's Tale*
	1876 Publication of *The Hand of Ethelberta*	**1876** Lewis Carroll, *The Hunting of the Snark*
	1876-8 Lives in Sturminster Newton	
1877 Queen Victoria assumes the title of Empress of India; Thomas Edison invents the phonograph	**1877** Publishes *The Return of the Native;* becomes a figure on the London literary scene	

World events	Hardy's life	Poetry
1879 Edison produces incandescent electric light	**1879** Birth of Florence Emily Dugdale	
1880-1 First Boer War in southern Africa, ending in defeat for the British	**1880-1** Publication of *The Trumpet Major;* bedridden, dictates *A Laodicean* to Emma	**1880** Tennyson, *Ballads and Other Poems*
1882 Death of Charles Darwin	**1882** Attends Darwin's funeral; publication of *Two on a Tower*	**1882** Swinburne, *Tristram of Lyonesse and Other Poems*
	1883 Moves to Dorchester; publishes *The Dorsetshire Labourer*	**1883** Robert Browning, *Jocoseria*
	1885 Moves into Max Gate (the house Hardy had designed himself)	**1885** Birth of Ezra Pound
	1886 Publication of *The Mayor of Casterbridge;* begins to plan epic *The Dynasts* about the Napoleonic Wars	**1886** Tennyson, *Locksley Hall, Sixty Years After;* death of William Barnes
	1887 Publication of *The Woodlanders;* visits Italy	**1887** George Meredith, *Ballads and Poems of Tragic Life*
1888 'Jack the Ripper' murders terrorise East London	**1888** Collection of short stories published as *Wessex Tales*	**1888** Birth of T.S. Eliot; death of Arnold
		1889 Death of Robert Browning
	1890 Death of Tryphena Sparks	
1891 Assisted Education Act makes elementary education free in England	**1891** Success and financial security follow *Tess of the d'Urbervilles;* marriage begins to deteriorate	
	1892 Death of Thomas Hardy's father; publishes *The Well-Beloved* in serial form	**1892** Death of Tennyson
	1893 Meets Florence Henniker in Dublin and becomes infatuated	
	1894 Publishes the collection of stories *Life's Little Ironies*	

World events	Hardy's life	Poetry
1895 The Lumière brothers patent the cinematograph; Wilhelm Roentgen experiments with X-rays	**1895** Public outrage follows publication of *Jude the Obscure*; marriage increasingly unhappy	**1895** William Butler Yeats, *Poems*; birth of Robert Graves
	1896 Abandons novels after reception of *Jude the Obscure*; devotes himself to poetry	**1896** A.E. Housman, *A Shropshire Lad*; birth of Edmund Blunden
	1898 Publishes *Wessex Poems and Other Verses*	**1898** Oscar Wilde, *The Ballad of Reading Gaol*
1899-1902 Second Boer War leads to control of southern Africa by the Boers	**1899** Publishes *Poems of the Past and Present*	**1899** Yeats, *The Wind Among the Reeds*
1901 Death of Queen Victoria; Guglielmo Marconi transmits radio signals across the Atlantic		**1901** Meredith, *A Reading of Life*
1903 Henry Ford founds his motor company	**1903** First volume of *The Dynasts* appears	
	1904 Meets Florence Dugdale; death of Thomas Hardy's mother	
	1906 Publication of *The Dynasts*, Part II	
		1907 Birth of W.H. Auden
1908 'Votes for Women' rally in Hyde Park, London	**1908** Publication of *The Dynasts*, Part III	**1908** Yeats, *Collected Works*
1909 Louis Blériot makes first cross-Channel flight	**1909** Publishes *Time's Laughingstocks and Other Verses*; succeeds George Meredith as President of the Society of Authors	**1909** Meredith, *Last Poems*; Ezra Pound, *Exultations and Personae*; death of Swinburne and Meredith
	1910 Awarded Order of Merit by King George V; Florence Dugdale lives at Max Gate as his secretary	**1910** Yeats, *Poems: Second Series*
1912 *Titanic* sinks with the loss of over 1,000 lives	**1912** Emma dies on 27 November; leads to the *Poems of 1912-13*	**1912** Pound, *Ripostes*

World events	Hardy's life	Poetry
	1913 Revisits Cornwall and Plymouth	
1914 Outbreak of First World War	**1914** Marries Florence; publishes *Satires of Circumstance, Lyrics and Reveries*	
	1915 Death of Thomas Hardy's sister Mary	**1915** Pound, *Cathay*
	1916 Publication of *Selected Poems*	
		1917 Robert Graves, *Fairies and Fusiliers;* death of Edward Thomas
1918 First World War ends, with over 8 million dead worldwide	**1918** Publishes *Moments of Vision and Miscellaneous Verses;* begins work on autobiography, *The Life of Thomas Hardy,* with Florence	**1918** Edward Thomas, *Last Poems*
	1919 Publication of *Collected Poems*	**1919** Siegfried Sassoon, *The War Poems*
	1920 Receives honorary degree from Oxford University	**1920** T.S. Eliot, *Poems;* Graves, *Country Sentiment*
	1922 Publishes *Late Lyrics and Earlier*	**1922** Eliot, *The Waste Land;* Edmund Blunden, *The Shepherd and Other Poems;* Yeats, *Later Poems;* birth of Philip Larkin
1923 Civil war in Russia ends with the Union of Soviet Socialist Republics	**1923** Prince of Wales visits Max Gate	**1923** Blunden, *To Nature*
1925 Creation of the British Broadcasting Corporation	**1925** Publication of *Human Shows, Far Phantasies, Songs and Trifles*	**1925** Pound, *A Draft of XVI Cantos;* Blunden, *English Poems;* Eliot, *Poems 1909-25*
1926 The General Strike in Britain		
	1928 Dies on 11 January; heart buried in Stinsford Churchyard, ashes in Westminster Abbey	**1928** Yeats, *The Tower;* Blunden, *Japanese Garland, Retreat and Winter Nights*
	1937 Death of Florence Hardy	

alienation the sense of being separated from, or adrift within, one's environment or social context

alliteration a sequence of repeated consonantal sounds in a stretch of language, e.g. the repeated 'r' sound in 'And the rotten rose is ript from the wall' ('During Wind and Rain'). The matching consonants are usually at the beginning of words or stressed syllables

allusion a passing reference in a work of literature to something outside itself (such as another work of literature, a legend, a cultural belief or a historical fact)

anapaest in English versification an anapaest is a trisyllabic metrical foot consisting of two unstressed syllables followed by a stressed syllable (ti-ti-tum). For example, 'When the Present has latched its postern behind my tremulous stay' is a hexameter with a combination of iambic and anapaestic feet

anthology a collection of works (usually poetry) by different authors

assonance the correspondence, or near-correspondence, in two words of the stressed vowel, and sometimes those which follow (but – unlike rhyme – not of the consonants). For example, 'The home-bound foot-folk wrap their snow-flaked heads' in 'The Five Students'. Assonance can be described as the vowel equivalent of alliteration

ballad a traditional poem or song which tells a story in simple, colloquial language. A ballad's story, which is often tragic in nature (as in Hardy's 'A Trampwoman's Tragedy'), is told through dialogue and action, while structural features typically include refrains and incremental repetition

ballad metre a quatrain of alternate four-stress and three-stress lines, usually roughly iambic, rhymed either abcb or abab (also known as common measure). 'The Oxen' uses this metre:

> Christmas Eve, and twelve of the clock.
>> 'Now they are all on their knees,'
> An elder said as we sat in a flock
>> By the embers in hearthside ease.

bathos a ludicrous descent from the elevated treatment of a subject to the dull and trivial

caesura (pl. **caesurae**) a pause within a line of poetry, caused by the natural organisation of the language into phrases, clauses and sentences, which do not conform to the natural metrical pattern. See, for example, 'At Castle Boterel':

> And to me, // though Time's unflinching rigour,
> In mindless rote, // has ruled from sight
> The substance now, // one phantom figure
> Remains on the slope, // as when that night
> Saw us alight.

colloquialism the use of the kinds of expression and grammar associated with ordinary, everyday speech rather than formal language

common measure another term for ballad metre

couplet a pair of consecutive lines of poetry which rhyme together

cycle a group of poems, plays, stories or novels which are grouped together, either by the author or by tradition, and which all deal, more or less, with some central theme or themes. See also elegy

dactyl in English versification, a type of metrical foot which consists of a strongly stressed syllable followed by two weak ones (tum-ti-ti), as in 'The Voice', where the line 'Woman much missed, how you call to me, call to me' is a dactylic tetrameter

dialect the particular style and manner of speaking of a specified area, nation or social class

diction the choice of words in a work of literature: the kind of vocabulary used

dimeter a line of poetry consisting of two metrical feet (i.e. two main stresses), for example the line 'And feeling fled' from 'At Castle Boterel'. Dimeters are rarely used except in conjunction with other line-lengths

double rhyme another term for feminine rhyme

dramatic monologue a specific kind of poem in which a single person, not the poet, is the 'speaker'

egotistical sublime a phrase used by John Keats (1795–1821) to describe what he considered to be the excessively self-centred quality of William Wordsworth's poetry

elegy a poem of lamentation, usually focusing on the death of a single person. More generally, the term 'elegy' can also be used to describe any gravely meditative work of poetry. Many elegies follow a conventional pattern, or cycle of sections meant to emulate the phases of mourning, which initially register shock at the death, followed by despair, resignation and, finally, reconciliation

epic a long narrative poem in an elevated style; typical epic themes include myth, legend, and the birth and destruction of nations

epigraph a quotation or fragment placed by a writer at the beginning of a poem, novel or chapter as a clue or hint towards its meaning

epitaph an inscription on a tomb, or a piece of writing suitable for that purpose

feminine ending a line of poetry which ends on an unstressed syllable (see metre). The following lines from 'The Going' have feminine endings, since the final syllables of 'follow' and 'swallow' are unstressed:

> Where I could not follow
> With wing of swallow

feminine rhyme rhymed words of two or more syllables, where the last syllable is not stressed (as in 'follow'/'swallow'); also known as double rhyme

foot in order to determine the metre of a line of poetry, it is necessary to divide it into feet, which are certain fixed combinations of weakly and strongly stressed syllables, such as anapaests, dactyls, iambs and trochees

free verse poetry released from the convention of metre. Although it can be very rhythmical, a poem in free verse cannot be resolved into the regular lines of repeated feet which characterise traditional versification. It was developed extensively in the twentieth century, particularly by modernists such as T.S. Eliot and Ezra Pound

heptameter a line of poetry consisting of seven metrical feet, i.e. seven main stresses, as in 'Their dawns bring lusty joys, it seems; their evenings all that is sweet' from 'In Tenebris II'

hexameter a line of poetry consisting of six metrical feet, i.e. six main stresses, as in 'The Immanent Will that stirs and urges everything' from 'The Convergence of the Twain'

iamb the commonest metrical foot in English versification, consisting of a weak stress followed by a strong stress (ti-tum). 'So fair a fancy few would weave' (from 'The Oxen') is an example of an iambic tetrameter

ideology the collection of ideas, opinions, values, beliefs and preconceptions which combine to make up the 'mind-set' of a group of people, that is, the intellectual framework through which they view everything, and which colours all their attitudes and feelings. The term is particularly used to refer to people's assumptions about power and authority

imagery in its narrowest sense an image is a picture in words – a description of some visible scene or object. More commonly, however, 'imagery' refers to the figurative language in a work of literature, such as metaphors and similes; or all the words which refer to objects and qualities which appeal to the senses and feelings

imagism a self-conscious literary movement in Britain and the United States initiated by Ezra Pound and T.E. Hulme around 1912. The imagists valued directness of language in short lyric poems, usually constructed around single images, and exploiting juxtaposition

impersonality the quality in literature of having no sense of the writer's personality and no personal tone or references

incremental repetition a term used to describe the use of a repeated refrain in poems, especially ballads, which is altered from one stanza to the next so as to fit in with the story or comment on the action. In 'The Five Students', for example, the fifth line of each stanza is a refrain, which is modified each time one of the characters is lost

internal rhyme a pair of words rhyming within a single line of poetry, rather than at two line-ends

irony a use of language, widespread in all kinds of literature and everyday speech, which is characterised by saying or writing one thing while another is meant

lament a poem expressing deep sorrow for the death of a person or people, or loss of status and security

long metre a quatrain in which each line has four stresses, usually iambic, and rhymed abcb, abab or aabb, as in the first stanza of 'Channel Firing':

> That night your great guns, unawares,
> Shook all our coffins as we lay,
> And broke the chancel window-squares,
> We thought it was the Judgment-day

lyric a poem, usually short, expressing in a personal manner the feelings and thoughts of an individual speaker

masculine ending a line of poetry which ends on a stressed syllable. This example, from 'At Castle Boterel', has alternating masculine and feminine endings:

Myself and a girlish form benighted
In dry March weather. We climb the road
Beside a chaise. We had just alighted
To ease the sturdy pony's load

masculine rhyme a monosyllabic rhyme on the final stressed syllables of two lines of poetry ('road'/'load' in the previous example)

melodrama although the word 'melodrama' can refer to a specific genre of sensationalist theatre, the term is used nowadays simply to describe any writing which is naïvely sensational or 'over the top', particularly from an emotional point of view

memoir an autobiography or a written account of one's memories, focusing on events witnessed and people known rather than on aspects of one's life and individuality

metaphor derived from the Greek meaning 'carrying over', the term 'metaphor' describes a departure from literal writing which goes further than a comparison (or simile) between two different things or ideas by fusing them together: one thing is described as being another thing, thus 'carrying over' all its associations. For example, in the last stanza of 'In Tenebris II' Hardy emphasises the threats to happiness ('delight') by describing it as a plant whose natural growth is 'cramped by crookedness, custom, and fear'

metre the pattern of stresses occurring (more or less regularly) in lines of poetry and arranged within a fixed total number of syllables (although a feminine ending is an accepted variation). In English poetry the metrical system is accentual–syllabic, in other words, both stressed and unstressed syllables are counted. Combinations of stressed and unstressed syllables are referred to as feet

modernism a term applied to experimental trends in literature (and other arts) in the early twentieth century; in poetry the reader is often challenged to deduce meaning from a collage of fragmentary images and complex allusions

motif a literary device, such as a theme, image or symbol, which recurs frequently, either within a body of literature or within a single work

Movement, the name for a group of poets of the 1950s whose work was collected in the anthology *New Lines* (1956) by Robert Conquest. Contributors included Philip Larkin, Thom Gunn, Ted Hughes and Elizabeth Jennings; they found common ground in a move away from the perceived excesses of modernism towards the poetic qualities of intelligence, control and verbal dexterity, combined with wit, clarity and a certain modesty of ambition

narrator the character (as distinct from the poet) in a ballad or other narrative poem who tells the story

neologism the coining of a new word; an innovation in language

objective correlative a term used by T.S. Eliot to describe an external equivalent for an internal state of mind. An objective correlative is thus any object, scene, event or situation that may be said to stand for or evoke a given mood or emotion, as opposed to a direct subjective expression of it

pathetic fallacy a term coined by John Ruskin to refer (pejoratively) to the attribution of human feelings to inanimate objects (i.e. a form of personification). Today the term is used, descriptively rather than negatively, to refer to the identification of a poet's own mood with the properties of the external world: to take a simple example, if the poet is sad, the weather may therefore be portrayed as gloomy. In 'A Death-Day Recalled' Hardy mocks this common poetic technique when he asks why 'Beeny [Cliff] did not quiver' on the day of Emma's death

pentameter a line of poetry consisting of five metrical feet, i.e. five main stresses. When these feet are basically iambic, the result is the commonest line form in English poetry, as in 'This candle-wax is shaping to a shroud' from 'Standing by the Mantelpiece'

periphrasis an indirect manner of describing, or speaking, also called circumlocution. For example, in 'A Death-Day Recalled' Hardy describes the tide at Pentargan Bay as the 'creamy surge'

persona (pl. **personae**) an identity assumed by a writer in a literary work (in Latin, a 'mask'): a means of writing from a perspective not one's own. See also impersonality

personification a variety of figurative or metaphorical language in which things or ideas are treated as if they were human beings, with human attributes and feelings. In 'The Five Students', for example, Hardy writes that 'The sun grows passionate-eyed'

Petrarchan sonnet a form of sonnet made up of an octave (a group of eight lines) and a sestet (a group of six lines) with the rhyme scheme abbaabba cdecde (or sometimes abbaabba cdcdcd)

prosody the science of versification: the study of the theory and development of metres and stanza forms

quatrain a stanza of four lines

refrain words or lines recurring at intervals in the course of a poem, sometimes with slight variation, usually at the end of a stanza; they are especially common in songs and ballads

rhetoric originally the art of speaking (and writing) effectively so as to persuade an audience; the term is now often used to cover the whole range of literary and linguistic devices. The term 'rhetorical question' is used to refer to a question asked not for the sake of enquiry but for emphasis, when the writer or speaker expects the reader or audience to be totally convinced about the appropriate reply

rhyme though by no means all verse is rhymed, rhyme is one of the most striking and obvious differences between verse and prose, and the most easily identified common aspect of English versification. It consists of chiming or matching sounds at the ends of lines of poetry, which create a very clearly audible sense of pattern

rhyme scheme the pattern of rhymes within a stanza or section of a poem, usually expressed by an alphabetical code (e.g. 'aabb') in which identical letters indicate the lines which rhyme

rhythm in English poetry and prose the chief element of rhythm is the variation in levels of stress accorded to the syllables in a particular stretch of language; in poetry the rhythm is more or less controlled and regular (see metre)

Romantic the 'r' is usually capitalised (as here) to distinguish the popular usage of the word 'romantic' from a convenient term of English literary history used to denote the period from 1789 (the French Revolution) to about 1830. Principal English Romantic writers included Wordsworth, Coleridge, Byron, Keats and Shelley. There are a large number of literary interests and attributes which may loosely be labelled 'Romantic', including: a concern to value feeling and emotion rather than the human capacity to reason; an interest in the primitive or the exotic (both geographically and historically); a conviction about the centrality of the individual; the discovery of a new relationship with nature; an appreciation of the value of the imagination; and a need for rebellion against 'rules', whether of literature or society at large

rondeau an elaborate verse form, French in origin and usually playful in subject matter. A rondeau typically consists of thirteen lines, employing only two rhymes, plus a refrain: the first word or opening phrase is repeated after the eighth and the thirteenth lines

simile a species of figurative writing involving a direct comparison of one thing to another. Similes typically make use of the words 'like' or 'as', for example 'The tangled bine-stems scored the sky, / Like strings of broken lyres' in 'The Darkling Thrush'

sonnet a lyric poem of fixed form: fourteen lines of iambic pentameter which are rhymed and organised according to one of several intricate schemes. They often comprise an octave (eight lines) and a sestet (six lines), or three quatrains and a couplet

stanza a unit of several lines of poetry; a repeated group of lines of poetry. What distinguishes a stanza from simply any section of poetry is the fact that it is a regular and repeated aspect of the poem's shape

stereotype a standard, fixed idea or mental impression; a cliché or stock character

stress in any word of more than one syllable, more emphasis or loudness will be given to one of the syllables in comparison with the others; in English poetry, the metre of a line is determined by regular patterns of stressed syllables in a sequence of stressed and unstressed syllables

symbol something which represents something else by analogy or association – a writer may use conventional symbols, which form part of a literary or cultural tradition, as well as creating new ones. For example, Hardy often viewed the railway as a symbol of nineteenth-century 'progress' in general: it is used in this way in 'The Pity of It', and, slightly differently, in 'Places', where the 'urgent clack' of the present day suggests the noise of a train passing along the track

syntax the grammatical structure of sentences

tetrameter a line of poetry consisting of four metrical feet, i.e. four main stresses, as in 'We stood by a pond that winter day' from 'Neutral Tones'

tragedy although technically 'tragedy' refers to a genre of drama, in general literary usage the term can refer to any work which traces the downfall of an individual, particularly if this downfall illustrates both the capacities and the limitations of human life

trimeter a line of poetry consisting of three metrical feet, i.e. three main stresses, as in 'In a solitude of the sea' from 'The Convergence of the Twain'

triple rhyme a rhyme on three syllables, for example 'listlessness' and 'wistlessness' in 'The Voice'

trochee in English versification a trochee is a foot consisting of a strongly stressed syllable followed by a weakly stressed syllable: 'Folk all fade. And whither' (from 'Exeunt Omnes') is a trochaic trimeter

verse form a repeated pattern in terms of line length, metre and rhyme of stanzas which compose a poem. This includes fixed poetic forms such as the sonnet, the rondeau, etc.

versification the study of the art of writing metrically (and with attention not only to metre, but rhythm, rhyme and stanza form); also, the act of composition of poetry

Victorian a term referring to the reign of Queen Victoria (1837–1901). It is often regarded as a homogeneous literary period, but in reality it manifested huge changes in society, outlook and literary output

Author of this note

Alan Pound is Head of the Department of English and Drama at St Martin's College in Lancaster. He has co-authored, with Mike Davis, *The Active Reader* (Simon and Schuster, 1992), a course book for English Key Stage 4, and co-edited, again with Mike Davis, *Blake: Selected Poems* (Heinemann, 1996).

Jane Austen
Emma

Louis de Bernières
Captain Corelli's Mandolin

Caryl Churchill
Top Girls and *Cloud Nine*

Charles Dickens
Bleak House

T.S. Eliot
The Waste Land

Homer
The Iliad

Aldous Huxley
Brave New World

Christopher Marlowe
Edward II

George Orwell
Nineteen Eighty-four

William Shakespeare
Henry IV Pt I

William Shakespeare
Henry IV Part II

William Shakespeare
Richard III

Tom Stoppard
Arcadia and *Rosencrantz and Guildenstern are Dead*

Virgil
The Aeneid

Jeanette Winterson
Oranges are Not the Only Fruit

Tennessee Williams
Cat on a Hot Tin Roof

Metaphysical Poets